Postcards from the Old Man

and

Other Correspondence

from Clearwater, Minnesota

Cynthia Anne Frank Stupnik

HERITAGE BOOKS
2008

HERITAGE BOOKS
AN IMPRINT OF HERITAGE BOOKS, INC.

Books, CDs, and more—Worldwide

For our listing of thousands of titles see our website
at
www.HeritageBooks.com

Published 2008 by
HERITAGE BOOKS, INC.
Publishing Division
100 Railroad Ave. #104
Westminster, Maryland 21157

Copyright © 2004 Cynthia Anne Frank Stupnik

Cover Artwork Copyright © 2004 Matt Stupnik

Other books by the author:

Steppes to Neu Odessa: Germans from Russia Who Settled in Odessa Township, Dakota Territory, 1872-1876
2nd edition

All rights reserved. No part of this book may be reproduced or transmitted in any form or by any means, electronic or mechanical, including photocopying, recording or by any information storage and retrieval system without written permission from the author, except for the inclusion of brief quotations in a review.

International Standard Book Number: 978-0-7884-2523-3

ȸȸȸȸ

This book is dedicated to my mother

Winifred Johnson Frank

whose love for history

and Clearwater's local characters

inspired me to create my own stories.

ȸȸȸȸ

TABLE OF CONTENTS

Preface

vii

Introduction

Early Navigation

1

Completing My Education

20

Pleasantly Situated

28

Smoke and Gossip

48

Between Snag and Shore

67

Anchored in the Stream

70

Learning the River

85

Drifting Logs

111

The Parting Chorus

134

PREFACE

I began this long journey of self-discovery during a rigorous and productive creative writing class in college. Over the years, I have entered many writing contests, even won a few awards, and sent some poems and essays off for publication. In addition to my shorter works, I have written two editions of *STEPPES TO NEU-ODESSA, Germans from Russia Who Settled in Odessa Township, Dakota Territory, 1872-1876*, a biographical history of ancestors and their friends who settled in Yankton County, South Dakota. But for many years, I had no vision, nor did I think I had enough material, to compile a book of my more personal and creative stories and poems.

Once I took a serious look at my stacks of handiwork, I came upon the idea of using Mark Twain's humor and wisdom, as well as some old postcards I had collected of the Mississippi and Clearwater rivers, as a unifying theme to tie together my anthology. In most cases, because each poem and story had been composed individually, when I began to compile them into some type of consecutive format, I found I had an overlap of information. I attempted to eliminate some of this, but in a number of situations, I felt that although the information seemed repetitive and out of chronological order, it could not be eliminated without hindering the meaning of the story or poem. Therefore, although readers can start from the beginning of the book and read to the end, this format will allow them to read a poem, story, or chapter individually. In addition, I have used a number of illustrative captions from Twain's *Life on the Mississippi*, his years learning the river as a riverboat pilot, as section headers and story titles. I have also borrowed a number of quotes that are derived from a variety of his written sources that are in the public domain as theme developers.

Mark Twain said, in *Life on the Mississippi*, "[. . .] writers of all kinds are manacled servants of the public. We write frankly and fearlessly but then we "modify" before we print." For this reason, while the poems and stories are loosely based on some truth, I have changed characters and some of the situations to protect innocent people. Any likenesses to specific people, either living or dead, are unintentional.

A DAUGHTER OF THE MIDDLE BORDER

Garland writes about my earthy grandmothers
who left eastern hamlets,
following their wander-lusting husbands
across Dakota prairies.

These petticoat farmers produced the manna,
feeding the men who grappled with the land.
But their own hunger was harder to stave off
without churches, schools, and *McClure's*.

North of Yankton, my youthful father tired of treeless plains,
left the rise and fall of the coteau.
Hankering after richer pastures,
he drifted east, sinking his spade in Minnesota's fields.

Years later, I, like my grandmothers,
trekked to Dakota to work alongside my spouse.
We tilled the land in a different way,
reclaiming their inheritance of Canaan's blessings.

While home for now may be inside this Harvey Dunn landscape--
azure skies, green-gold desert, and pasque flowers—
I feel Twain's anchor, Old Man River,
tugging at my veins.

INTRODUCTION

A wannigan on the Mississippi River at Clearwater

"When I find a well-drawn character in fiction or biography I generally take a warm personal interest in him, for the reason that I have known him before—met him on the river."
-- Mark Twain, *Life on the Mississippi* --

The north side of Clearwater where the Clearwater River flows into the Mississippi

POSTCARD FROM THE OLD MAN

Lake Itasca-
Black loons skim my rock-line banks,
sip their sacrament to April days,
sing solemn psalms to my rhythmic beat.
On the horizon that barnacles sea to sky,
white gulls extend their sails, scoop my shores.
Brawny birches wave bon voyage
as I trickle forth in a silver stream . . .
                traveling light.

I pick up hitchhiking streams along the way.
Paddling past St. Cloud,
I swoosh by clumps of pussy willows,
growing alongside lilacs and wild plum in white blossom.
Clearwater River's mouth opens wide,
sending rippled yawns in my direction.

May 6th . . . male toads begin their trill,
calling for mates to meet by marshy milkweeds.
Sleek, black muskrats dive,
flapping their tails at anglers
casting lines from my clay-packed beaches.
Not much further before I plunge
on my muddy descent. . .
        Hannibal, St. Louis, New Orleans. . .

Having a good time-
Wish you were here.

> **"Man's mind clumsily and tediously and laboriously patches little trivialities together and gets a result – such as it is."**
> -- Mark Twain, *The Mysterious Stranger* --

After I graduated from high school, I couldn't wait to escape from this tiny town. Even though I had a good family and many close friends, Clearwater stifled me. Like Huck Finn, I hopped on my raft to "light out for the territory." In reality, I only moved as far away as Minneapolis and into a cozy apartment with other Clearwater girls who were also yearning for freedom and independence.

Even though I came back home many times before I married and left for good, wherever I have lived--Mississippi, Oregon, South Dakota--I often became caught up in waves of homesickness. But not until I started teaching *The Adventures of Huckleberry Finn* to my high school students did I realize that I was a child of the Old Man and anchored to this neck of the Mississippi River.

Clearwater, like many of the river towns Mark Twain writes about, has been made up of saints and scoundrels and others of varying fathoms in between. When I reflect on Clearwater's history and its notable and not so notable characters, I wonder what Twain, the great Wisecracker, would have said if he'd ever come this far north. Would he have been cynical of the town's stagnation since it lost its opportunity to become a major commercial center back in the 1800s? Would he have developed a few of the town drunks or regular visiting train bums into central characters for one of his famous novels? It is hard to say. But Clearwater, like many small river towns, has many stories waiting to be told.

The poems and essays in this book are about the type of individuals, situations, and places that impressed me as I grew up. And like Mark Twain, who Huck states "told the truth, mainly," except for those "things which he stretched," occasionally this author makes murky illusions to the past.

Postcards from the Old Man

EARLY NAVIGATION

The junction where Clearwater River flows into the Mississippi

"You can find in a text whatever you bring, if you will stand between it and the mirror of your imagination."
-- Mark Twain, "A Fable" --

Early Navigation

Clearwater's early zenith had long passed by the 1950's when my parents, older brother Don, and I moved into the area from St. Cloud. Kniss' Grocery, Anderson's Variety, Tri-County Lumber, West's Hardware, Judd Bentley's gas station, and the mortuary, stretching from north to south on Main Street, stood in the shadows of what this town used to be. Our move started my emotional ebb and flow for the countryside and historic town that sat on the edge of the Mississippi.

We lived a mile or so north of the small village, a short driveway up from Highway 152. Mom and Dad referred to it as the Allen place. Not a particularly well-maintained property, the house's siding had turned nearly gray for want of paint, but the cheap rent enticed my hardworking parents.

The rental had other features that sometimes provided our family with story material. The large front lawn spread out nicely for a game of softball, tag, or croquet. A red-sided chicken coop stood to the side. Here Mom and Dad occasionally raised chickens for butchering. With hatchet in hand, Dad ran after the scattering and squawking birds, grabbed one by the legs, carried it over to the tree stump, and whacked off its head. The headless creature joined others in a death march as blood spurted from its neck. Once the soldier quit flopping, Mom picked it up by its shank and dipped it in a pail of boiling water to loosen its feathers. The combined smells of scalded down, flesh, and blood caused my stomach to flip. From that day forward, the smell of chicken soup makes me nauseous.

Although Dad seldom used the lean-to in the back of the house for anything besides storing coal and wood for the stoves, my brother used it for his own entertainment. Once he and a friend, Betty, decided the vast yard and the woods didn't offer them enough places for their adventures. They climbed the tree and swung over to the lean-to's sloping roof. They giggled as they scrambled to the peak and sat looking at the cornfield, the highway, and the neighbors' houses.

When they tired of their fun, they attempted to get down but found that they were more than up a stump. In the first place, no matter how he stretched, Don couldn't reach the tree limb that they had used to swing over onto the roof. He scooted on his butt to the roof's edge. But he realized he was too far up to jump to the ground. In unison, Betty and Don laughed and screemed, "Mom! Help!" "Winnie! Help!"

Mom went outside to investigate the noise. When she saw them on the roof, she shrieked, "What the . . .? How did you get up there? I suppose you don't know how you'll get down now either?"

Matter of fact, neither of these "lamebrains" had thought much about anything except having fun. What was she going to do? Dad was at work like most of the men who lived in the area. She thought of the farmer who lived about a half mile away. She called his wife who said she'd send Theo right down. Whatever Mom said to Don and Betty before he arrived made them wonder if they were more in danger staying on the roof or facing her once they stepped on the ground.

The front yard offered many places for adventure but so did the backyard. A worn path sloped from the back of the house and led to an old barn and rickety fence that housed pigs. Don was always looking for fun things to do. Once he crawled in the pigsty and hopped on one of the dirty-pink creatures. The animal became so startled it ran sideways, kicking and crashing into the other piglets. Don managed to stay on the bucking porker for a few seconds. Once he landed, though, he found himself sitting in a fresh pile of manure. As he sat there, his cries for help blended with the cacophony of squeals from the herd.

While this hobby farm's outside surroundings offered a variety of places for daily activities, the run-down charm on the inside of the house provided solitude. The shaded front porch with hanging grapevines kept us cool in the summer. On hot afternoons when Don and I came in to cool down from the sun, we fought over whose turn it was to sit in Dad's wicker rocker in the corner of the porch. Of course, when Dad got home from work, he extinguished the flaming fights and took over as the resident rocker. While reading the *St. Cloud Daily Times*, he sat with his right leg propped up and hanging over the arm of the chair. Mom hollered at him about this because the chair had belonged to her grandparents. The chair may not have been worth much in cost, but it was rich in memory.

Bare of cupboards, the kitchen contained a hodgepodge of furniture and appliances; these, along with the paint and wallpaper, offered a half-century's view of décor and domesticity, minus the butter churn. Tin squares covered the ceiling. A nickel-plated wood stove, leaning against one of the yellow walls, kept us warm in the winter. The floor displayed the blue and yellow checkered linoleum Mom had purchased with her first paycheck from Metzroth's where she worked in the tailoring department. Red vinyl and chrome chairs sat around the gray Formica table. A white and turquoise, combination wringer-washer-dishwasher stood next to the white 1940's Kelvinator refrigerator. In between the window and the door to the summer kitchen that we never used stood the white kitchen range.

Here I once decided to help Mom make supper. While she was taking a nap, I painstakingly peeled potatoes, washing them carefully to remove all the dirt. I cut them up, put the chunks in a pot and placed a cover on top, like I had seen her do many times. I slid the pot on the burner and went outside to play. Before long, I heard Mom yelling. When I entered the smoke-filled kitchen, I saw her pouring water into the pan, creating sizzling steam.

"What did you do? What did you do?"

I told her I was "just trying to help." I looked inside the pot and saw coal-like potatoes.

She scolded, "First, young lady, you needed to add water to the potatoes in order to get them boiling. Second, you have NO BUSINESS playing with the stove without me watching you. You could have been burned very badly!"

I figured Mom was concerned about my welfare, but I also learned "money didn't grow on trees" because she had to throw away the potatoes and the pot.

Postcards from the Old Man

A pantry off the kitchen contained many surprises. A trap door on the floor opened to the cellar. Little more than a black hole, this clammy dark place was the source of the mice for which Dad had to set many mousetraps in the spring and fall. Even though the mice scared me, the little room kept me entertained on raining days. The edibles that lined the shelves reminded me of a storehouse. I often played that I was a clerk at Kniss'Grocery. I organized the shelves, restacking red and white cans of Campbell soups, white bags of flour and sugar, and boxes of Cheerios, Wheaties, Frosted Flakes, and Nabisco saltines. I wrote out sales slips for make-believe customers and made change for them with Monopoly money.

Once I chose the breadbox in which to hide my black patent leather shoes that I wore only on Sundays and for special occasions. One morning before we left for church, I came down from my bedroom and told Mom I couldn't find my good shoes, hoping I'd get new ones because these pinched my toes and squeaked when I walked. She threatened, "You'd better find them, young lady!" With that command, I pretended to search the house. I looked under my bed, under Don's bed, in my toy box, and in my closet beneath the fallen stacks of clothes.

I braved Mom's temper again when I went downstairs and told her that I still couldn't find them. This time she sent Dad to help me with my search. After this proved fruitless, Mom said I'd have to wear my sneakers to Sunday School because they couldn't afford to buy me new ones.

Embarrassed to wear dirty red Keds to church, I snuck into the pantry and pulled my good ones from the bread box. "Hey, hey!" I shouted. "I found them!" Of course, I hadn't thought enough ahead to explain where the shoes had been the whole time. Finally, I fessed up that I had hidden them because they made noise when I walked and they hurt my feet. Dad told me to put them on. He leaned down and squeezed the sides and squished the toes with his thumb. He decided that yes, they indeed had become too small, but I'd have to "tough it out" and wear them this day. He promised he'd come up with the money to buy me a new pair soon. I may or may not have prayed for new shoes that Sunday, but as I sat in church listening to the

Early Navigation

minister's long sermon, I slipped off my shoes and dreamed of wearing brown penny loafers with shiny copper pennies like those pictured in the Ward's catalog.

But there were other fascinating rooms in this old house. The living room had a bay window that faced the front lawn and offered a cozy, Victorian nook. Every year, we placed our Christmas tree here, and Don and I etched yuletide designs of snowmen, Santa, and reindeer on the frosted squares of glass. Sometimes I played ghost behind the lace curtains. Othertimes, I watched trucks and cars spray white or brown clouds as they plowed through snow drifts or swerved in mounds of loose sand.

In the mid-fifties, the folks ordered their first television and decided it would fit nicely in this window area. One evening, after Dad came home from work at the Granite City Iron Works in St. Cloud, the whole family took a trip into town to pick up the set at the train depot. When we got it home, Dad and our neighbor Ray unloaded the mahogany wood model from the Montgomery Ward's packing box. They hauled it to the window and plugged it in. Then they climbed the ladder to the roof and carefully walked to the antenna that they had mounted a few days before.

Postcards from the Old Man

The rest of us were assigned duties. Don stood at the bottom of the ladder repeating the questions the two men asked: "How does the picture look now?" Mom stood in front of the set and watched the black and white test pattern. I stood at the door and repeated her answers to Don who hollered them back up to the men: "Turn the antenna a little more to the left" or "Turn it more to the right" until the picture looked straight and she said, "It's good right now."

Once Dad came back into the house and made a few adjustments in the back of the television Mom turned the dial. The first picture I saw was of Mickey Mouse. Since it was after six o'clock, she went to the kitchen to finish making supper. Dad thanked Ray for his help before he headed to the bathroom to take his evening bath. And Don and I lay down on the floor and watched Annette, Bobbie, Jimmy, Donald Duck, and the rest of the Mickey Mouse Club crew.

The place had indoor plumbing but no hot water heater, and while we appreciated the running water from late spring to early fall, winter brought its own problems. Mom always had to heat water for washing clothes and doing dishes. But in the winter, because the house had little insulation, we had to keep the sink and tub faucets running, otherwise, the pipes would freeze. Nor could we take baths in the tub because once it turned cold outside, the drain would freeze shut. Late on Saturday afternoons Mom and Dad set canners of water to heat on the kitchen range and then poured the heated water into the old metal washtub they had placed in front of the stove in the living room. We all took turns scrubbing in the tub. Mom and Dad dumped the water out after each bath and then poured new water in for the next person. When it was time for Dad's bath, I couldn't understand how he fit in that tub.

Mom and Dad slept in the only bedroom downstairs, but the upstairs housed more bedrooms. My tiny room was at the top of the steps. Previous tenants had papered it with red drums and brown teddy bears on a background of beige. Taking up one wall was a huge walnut wardrobe with glass doorknobs where I kept my clothes—skirts and blouses, jumpers, Sunday dresses, shoes--and of course, my collection of bride and baby dolls. On clear black nights, after I crawled into bed and either Mom or Dad kissed me goodnight, I gazed out the window, counted the stars in the blackening sky and watched the moon like a beacon come up over the barn in the backyard.

The pipe from the coal stove, which often turned red-hot in winter, came up through my brother's bedroom where he slept in an iron-framed bed with a thin sagging mattress. On terribly cold nights, I often joined him in his bed and we cuddled under the quilts to stay warm. While we attempted to fall asleep, we heard Mom and Dad talking quietly below us and the low hum from the televison--*Arthur Godfrey and His Talent Scouts* or *The Thin Man*.

The guest room, with its sloping ceiling, had the most wonderful closet hidden behind a curtain. My mother used this as a storage area for cardboard boxes full of Christmas ornaments, old coats smelling of mothballs, and stacks of tattered *LIFE* and *LOOK* magazines. My brother and I loved making our grand entrances as actors or magicians from behind the curtain. Don wore an old black hat, tied a bath towel to his shoulders and played hocus pocus, pretending to cut me in half. I donned one of Mom's castoff dresses, stepped into her open-toed heels. With my hand placed on my chest, I screeched out high notes, pretending I was a famous opera star.

My brother, five years my senior, and I often played together because we had few neighborhood children to play with. And while Donald and I often did not get along, we occasionally understood each other in a few important matters.

From time to time, we had a gathering of pets. One of the first animals we helped care for was a German Shepherd that came on loan from our uncle Dick who could not have a dog in his St. Paul apartment. The dog had the ability to get into the center of a group of people as they talked. He turned his head to each speaker and wagged his tail as though he understood what the person was saying. His antics kept us laughing. Unfortunately, the dog's incessant need to chase cars brought his visiting days to a premature stop.

Once our father brought home a brown and white-faced calf for us to help raise. This creature was a novelty that Donald and I named

Postcards from the Old Man

Poncho. We willingly fed and pet our new friend every morning before school. The calf grew to a good-sized steer and seemed content staked in the field by the driveway.

One morning before heading off to school, Donald filled the bucket with corn and headed out to the yard. He came back in and told Mom that he couldn't find Poncho. She told us said that our neighbor George had come by early that morning with his truck and had taken the steer into town. Neither my brother nor I analyzed the situation too deeply. I know I didn't give Poncho a thought as I sat behind my desk reading about Alice, Jerry, and Jip. Days went by and Don and I forgot about our pet.

One evening, as I set the table with plates, silverware, and glasses, Mom told me that we were having a treat for supper. I was to watch for Dad to drive in the yard from work and then she'd put the meat in the frying pan.

After Dad washed up for supper, he and Don pulled their chairs out from the table and began to pile their plates with heaping spoonfuls of creamy mashed potatoes and green beans with sprinkles of bacon. Mom had surely outdone herself. I handed her our plates so she could serve up the sizzling slabs of steak.

After grace, Dad offered to cut my meat, but I looked down at the red-brown liquid flowing into my innocent white potatoes and cried "Eeeew."

"What's the matter?" Dad asked.

"Can I have a bowl of Cheerios?"

"NO! After all the time and money we have spent on raising that calf…"

"Harold! We weren't going to say anything, remember?"

Donald and I looked down into our plates.

Early Navigation

"Poncho?" I asked and then felt the bile build up in the back of my throat and my eyes begin to water.

Because "people were starving in China," my brother and I sat at the table for quite awhile that night staring at our parents' bloody offering. But because they wanted to go to bed sometime that night, we were offered bowls of cereal so we wouldn't starve before morning. While we listened to Dad preach about good food getting thrown in the garbage, Mom reassured us that what wasn't eaten would be cut up for the next night's stew. Don and I knew that no gravy in the world could possibly cover up the fact that we'd eventually have to eat our pet.

We had other pets. Like most families, our cats helped with the mouse population. I didn't befriend many of these balls of fur, but Donald and I shared the responsibility for a few of them.

THE GUNNY SACK

My brother and I tried motherhood
after Big Momma, carrying one of her babes in her mouth,
got run over by a black car speeding in front of our house.
We nursed her kids with doll bottles
filled with warm skimmed milk.

They reminded me of Dracula—
tiny mouths, white-pointed teeth and blood-red tongues
as they wailed for more droplets of our breastless brew.
But their nourishment digested into a greenish mess.

When Dad had had enough of our charity,
he called for the neighbor
who grabbed our three, scraggly gray kittens,
and tossed them into the musty burlap bag
that flopped back and forth against his hip as he thumped away.
Squeaky meows grew faint as he left muddy footprints in the grass.

Dad's verdict seemed harsh,
but he had no money for a vet to tell him the inevitable--
nor could he do what our neighbor could do.

Early Navigation

But for me, the Allen place held other charms. Carol, the landlord's granddaughter, came to live in the small white house with blue trim at the other end of the driveway. We became best friends and seldom went a day without seeing each other. Sometimes on warm summer afternoons, she and I played in our hideout, resting against the large rock inside a little weedy alcove by the side of our house. Here we baked mud cakes using the chipped cups our mothers handed down to us.

Carol and Cindy in the hideout at the Allen place

Other times, because Mom and Dad had decided not to raise chickens for butchering anymore, we converted the chicken coop into a playhouse. With my red and white table and chair set, a peach-box cupboard filled with blue-speckled play dishes, and cradles and strollers loaded with stuffed bears and dolls, Carol and I created a world of make-believe. When we tired of the rock and the playhouse, we rode our trikes to her place, hopped on rusty Rocket Racer scooters, or pulled her baby brother, Joey, around the driveway in the red Radio Flyer wagon.

Our days for innocent play came to a pause when it was time for us to start first grade. Dressed in nearly identical blue-plaid dresses and armed with red-plaid lunch pails, we stood at the end of her driveway waiting for the orange bus with the words Clearwater Public School—District 742 to roll down 152 after dropping off big kids at either the junior or senior high schools in St. Cloud. After pulling the bi-fold door open, Al Abeln greeted us each morning with with a smile that shined brightly because of a silver-capped front tooth. For twelve years, he was our guard and guardian, watching our every move from his rearview mirror, reminding John to sit down when the bus was in motion, Jim to move over so Sylvester could scoot in, and Tom to quit teasing the girls.

During my first two or three years of attending the Clearwater school, we country kids rode only the morning bus because in the afternoons Mr. Abeln picked up the high school students in St. Cloud and brought them back to Clearwater. Consequently, after the bell rang at 3:30, Carol and I walked the mile and a half home. We often took the shortcut over the sandy beach where the pulp mill once stood by the Mill Pond, up the narrow trail that wound its way to the car path that ran through the Sportsmen's Park, and to the gravel road that ran in front of my house a half mile north.

Although we knew our folks expected us to come home right away, we often became sidetracked. One of our diversions was playing tag at Acacia Cemetery.

SUMMER'S PLAYGROUND

"You're it!"
screeched my red-headed friend,
as she whacked me on the back
where I hid behind the Stevens' tomb.

I leaned my forehead
against the knobby-barked oak.
The tree's canopy of arched branches
and coiled tendrils clutched the Shaws.
"One thousand one,
one thousand two,
one thousand three," I hollered.

Acacia shadows lurked behind Porters,
crawled over Sheldons,
crept across shrouded grass and acorn pyres,
tagging my friend before I reached "ready or not."

Like most children, I loved Christmas and waited each year for its surprises. After Thanksgiving, Mom spruced up the house, pulling out the boxes hidden in the upstairs closet. She scotch-taped greeting cards with snowy scenes, three kings on camels or green wreaths with red bows, on the living room doorway. For weeks, the house smelled of spicy fruitcake and vanilla and sugar cookies.

But home wasn't the only place we celebrated this loved holiday. My brother and I participated in traditional Sunday School programs where we sang, recited Bible verses, and exchanged puzzles and coloring books with other Sunday schoolers.

We participated in the school's Christmas programs as well. In first grade, I dressed up to resemble a pink-cheeked doll a young girl might receive for a present. In third or fourth grade my class played "Jingle Bells" and "Frosty the Snowman" on our flutephones. Some of us became candles when we slid into blue, yellow, or red plastic tubes that T&O Plastics had molded for the program.

Early Navigation

Around December 14, Dad, and sometimes the rest of our family, went to find our tree. For years, we went into town and bought from Ellis Kniss at the Kniss' Fairway Store. Because the branches were wrapped and wired and often covered in snow, we were always surprised with what we had purchased once we got home and began to unwrap our symbol of yuletide cheer.

THE FOUNDLINGS

My father's search to find our tree
would often take him out to see
if they would have at Kniss' Store
a Christmas tree like years before.

Up against the mart's north wall
stood evergreens so lush and tall.
But on the ground my dad detected
a scrub—discarded and neglected.

A tree to touch his tender heart—
for orphaned man, his counterpart.
He dragged it home where we awaited
a tree to love—when decorated.

As it stood in stand, we realized
the tree was less than he'd surmised.
The bells and balls, a garland rope
just didn't help. We gave up hope.

Out of ornaments; so what to do?
We finally admitted we were through.
Tinseled and lit, a star on top
that dried up tree was still a flop.

Now years later…in memory,
I think that I shall never see
a poem as ugly as that tree—
or one that means so much to me.

Not until years later, after I had married and left home for good, did I begin to understand the truth of Christmas and the joy of childhood innocence.

THE MAGIC BAG

In an insane attempt to get some Christmas shopping done early, I took off to the shopping mall the day after Thanksgiving. Wandering shoppers, full of yuletide spirit, bumped into each other, smiled politely, and said, "Excuse me." Smiling clerks cheerfully reminded their customers to "make sure you keep your receipt if you want to return this."

I knew that later in the season when shoppers rushed to finish their buying and clerks grew weary with the crazy hours and demands, the merry mood in the mall would change. As I was pushed from one end of the mall to the other, I saw grown-ups and children standing in a long line. Once up close, I watched a young child, a curly brown-haired girl--maybe three or four years old, crawl onto Santa's lap. I observed this nouveau man in his too-red suit and flat belly that made him look like he was just taking time out from his racquet ball game at the local YMCA. I remembered how I first met the man my small, German community called St. Nick.

It was a typical night in our pre-women's lib household. My ten-year-old brother Donnie stretched out on the floor to watch "Howdy Doody." Dad, sitting in the big rocking chair with his right leg hanging over the arm, read the evening newspaper. Mother washed the dishes and dipped them in clean water to rinse as I stood on a chair and wiped them dry with a white kitchen towel. This night, though, I didn't dilly-dally because I knew that company was arriving soon.

After I hung up the towel to dry, I ran to the living room window and peered out just in time to see two headlights beam into the driveway. No Dasher, no Dancer, no Prancer, no Vixen, just a '57 Studebaker station wagon screeching to a stop.

"They're here," I shouted.

Early Navigation

"Big hairy deal," Donnie mumbled and stared at the TV with his chin cupped in his hands.

How could he just lie there? Didn't he remember what happened last year?

I rehearsed softly, "I want a Tiny Tears and a Betty Crocker Bake Set. I want a Tiny Tears and a Betty Crocker Bake Set."

Soon I heard the porch screen door slam shut followed by a loud pounding on the door. Dad laughed, but hid behind the newspaper. Mom wiped out the dishpan. Apparently, they weren't going to make a move to let in the visitors. Without being invited, a red-suited man with a pointed red hat, red blobs on his cheeks and a short, white beard opened the door and walked in. Behind him, brandishing a snake-like whip walked a big man. Black soot covered the man's face and his baggy, brown suit. V-shaped eyebrows rimmed his dark, beady eyes.

The man in red, St. Nick, looked in my direction and roared, "Have you been a good little girl?"

I walked over and stood beside Mother. I wanted desperately to hide my face in Mother's apron just so I couldn't see their faces staring down at me, but I knew I was too old for that. Mother smoothed my dark brown ringlets, nodded, and smiled reassuringly at me.

I looked up as the old red man boomed, "Then what do you want Santa to bring you for Christmas?"

I swallowed hard and babbled, "Atinytearsandabettycrockerbakeset," in one long breath.

"Help your mother; obey your father; don't pout; don't cry. Then St. Nick will see what he can do. Remember, I'll be keeping an eye on you."

Out of a big brown sack, that magic bag, the scary man with the black soot on his face pulled a small, paper bag bunched in the middle. He handed it to me. Quickly, I reached out and snatched it out from the black, gloved hand before he could grab me. After I said "Thank you," I peeked into the bag, smelling peanuts and spicy candy ribbons. I saw a couple of chocolate drops on the top.

"Donald!" bellowed St. Nick. "Stand up here!"

I half hid behind my mother as I peeked at my brother.

"Ah, I don't believe in you anymore. You're a fake," Donald muttered.

Oh no, I thought, here we go again.

The man in brown growled and snapped his whip. Grabbing my brother by his back belt loop, he shoved him in the big brown sack.

I knew that sack had magic powers. It held everything--candy for good children, charcoal for bad. I knew that my brother was in that bag smothered in charcoal, yet Dad just sat in his chair laughing and reading the paper. Mom stood there with her hand covering her mouth. Neither made a move to help my brother.

"Let me out of here. You're stupid!"

The devilish man untwisted the sack, snapped his long, shiny, black whip and growled as Donnie jumped out. I looked at my brother, except for a very red face and sweat on his forehead, he looked all right--no soot! He didn't run to Dad or Mom; he just stood there looking at the floor.

"I thought you had learned last year, young man. This is a warning. You'd better watch yourself or there will be nothing under the tree for you this year."

With another snap of the whip, the sooty man thrust another candy-filled bag at Donnie. Then growling and snapping, the two visitors stomped out the door, hollering, "Ho, Ho, Ho!"

I still remember the too-sweet taste of the chocolate drops I ate after our visitors left. Although I do remember receiving the Betty Crocker Bake Set that year, I can't remember if I received the Tiny Tears or if Donnie was "good."

Mostly, I remember the dual nature of the holidays--the joyous expectation mixed with dread. Those same dualities have remained. Every Christmas I look forward to buying one new tree ornament, drinking egg nog, and singing old carols with my friends and family. But I dread the crowded stores, the hard gift decisions, and baking and frosting cookies. For me, Christmas will always be a magic bag--

Early Navigation

full of good and bad. Each year I hope for its wonderful gifts--while its demons lurk, waiting.

COMPLETING MY EDUCATION

Clearwater School and Congregational Church

"The difference between the almost right word & the right word is really a large matter--it's the difference between the lightning bug and the lightning."
-- Mark Twain, Letter to George Bainton--

Completing My Education

Chalk Dust

Since 1871, a two-story, brown school building has stood on the top of a hill overlooking the village of Clearwater. In the early years, students and teachers saw the murky Mississippi nuzzling peacefully by the town's shores. But when I started school, the trees stood so tall and the branches were so thick and heavy that the St. Luke's Catholic Church steeple was the only object we saw. The school bell's clanging summons for school to start never changed though. Students dropped baseballs and bats, picked up marbles, and leaned splintery, wooden stilts against the side of the building before they walked, not ran, through the hallways to arrive in their classrooms by 8:25. Inside the school's imposing walls, youngsters learned not only the three R's, but to say "excuse me" when walking between other people, and to raise one or two fingers for permission to go to the bathroom. For eight years I walked the creaky wooden floors, sat in the initial-scarred desks, obeyed matronly female teachers, and played hopscotch on the front sidewalk. As imperceptibly as chalk dust collecting in the blackboard ledge, I grew in size and knowledge.

In September 1956, as Janitor Hanson raised the flag to the top of the pole, my friend Carol and I entered the doors of the first and second grade classroom. We both wore the blue-and-red plaid dresses our mothers had made. I carried an oval plaid lunch box containing a peanut butter and grape jelly sandwich, an apple, a couple of chocolate chip cookies, and a plaid thermos filled with milk. Wearing black, horn-rimmed glasses and gray hair, Mrs. Freed welcomed us and showed us to our desk. She was thin, but soft and encouraging like a grandmother should be.

Three more students, David, Brian, and Barb, were added to our class. From that first day, the five of us stuck together, proud that we were the smallest group to attend the school. None of us liked it when other children joined our group. In fact, we secretly cheered when the newcomers moved out of town or teachers held them back.

Postcards from the Old Man

Every morning we stood beside our desks and said, "Good Morning, Mrs. Freed." After smiling and returning our greeting, she turned to the flag by the door, placed her hand over her heart, and led us, phrase by phrase in the recitation of the "Pledge of Allegiance."

She taught us the funny words to songs like "Ole' Dan Tucker" who brushed his teeth in a frying pan. While our heads hung to the side of our desks, we heard the wind blow as we sang "Down in the Valley."

With the help of Alice, Jerry, and Jip we learned to read. Three-inch flashcards, with pictures of apples and oranges, showed us that two plus two equals four. In the Red Chief lined notebooks we practiced printing our ABC's.

We also learned how to dance. Gingerly holding the outside of the shiny black record of *Famous Folkdances for Grade School Children,* Mrs. Freed placed it on the phonograph. Girls curtsied before grabbing hold of an unworthy boy's sweaty hands for the Virginia Reel. Occasionally, Mrs. Freed allowed us girls to dance the schottische without the boys. We'd formed a group of four, two in front and two in back, heeling and toeing our way left and right. The boys stood on the sides and laughed as we stumbled and tripped over each other's feet, especially when it was time for the front partners to swirl around and move to the back at the same time the back partners moved to the front.

Mrs. Freed, who gave gentle hugs and encouraging words, smelled like roses. Freckles covered her arms (not until I was older would I know that some were age spots). But she had rules: line up for recess; eyes on your own paper; no talking during study time. More than once I had the small hairs under my pig tails pulled for whispering to Carol. One time Steven, a second grader who sat behind me, tied my long braid around the inkwell. When I leaned forward, pain shot through my scalp. I squealed, "Ow!" Calling me to her desk, Mrs. Freed told me to hold out my hand. With her wooden rule, she whacked my hand five times. The sting of my palm was nothing compared to the sting of shame. Even though Steven had put his face down on the desk giggling, I didn't tattle on him. For no matter what the rules were in Mrs. Freed's room, when she said for us to be quiet, she meant it.

When I first laid eyes on Kurt, I loved him. He was another second grader who sat on the right side of Mrs. Freed's room. He had blue eyes, a cowlick in the back of his blonde hair, and a wide smile that showed an adorable split between his two front teeth. One day, as we walked home from school, I made a bargain with him. If he would kiss me, I would give him my new telescope. I took off my glasses, expecting our lips to lock. Instead, I felt a light brush of air as his lips escaped my pucker before he jerked the telescope out of my hands and ran for home.

None of us was eager to enter the third and fourth grades because of Mrs. Oatman, the freckled lady that other students nicknamed "Oatmeal" was in charge. In her room, we learned cursive handwriting from the green posters that hung on the wall. She stressed that a person with good penmanship used her whole arm to write, not just her wrist. With chalk clasped between her thumb and first two fingers, she wound up like a pitcher throwing a fast ball. The skin on her right upper arm flapped back and forth as she copied A through Z on the blackboard. As we practiced our alphabet during morning and afternoon sessions, she marshaled our progress by patrolling the aisles and bending over our desks, making suggestions on how to improve the curves of our capital S's and the tail-dips of our little f's. My fingers got sore and tired pinching the pencil point, so no matter how hard I tried, my letters always fell on top of each. My report card usually informed my parents of my progress: "Penmanship: Needs Improvement."

Mrs. Oatman also taught us musical appreciation through the flutephone. Every day we whistled and screeched on these plastic and beige, eight-holed horns trying to learn our scales. Somehow by December, we were ready for the all-school Christmas program. After we climbed the steps of the stage, Mrs. Oatman lined us up. While Santa (usually an upper classman from the eighth grade) and his elves (first or second grader boys and girls) stood by the Christmas tree, we squealed simple versions of "Frosty" and "Jingle Bells" for an audience of smiling parents.

I faced more challenges in third grade. One day the school brought in specialists to test students' hearing and eyesight. My poor eyesight due to a lazy left eye surprised no one; I had worn patches and glasses since two. But after the hearing test, Mrs. Oatman called my mother at home. Mom didn't drive, but our neighbor Alvina drove Mom into town so she could talk to the technician.

During recess, when I would have rather been outside playing Red Rover, the woman in white placed the headset back on my ears and rotated the black knobs of the brown box. I said, "Now," when I heard the high and low moans in my left ear. I waited for her to turn up the dial so I could hear the noise in my right ear. After a couple minutes, she lifted off the headset and looked at both Mother and my teacher. Mrs. Oatman patted me on the shoulder before she excused herself to go back to our classroom.

My mother asked, "Now what do we do?" The technician explained that Mom needed to make an appointment with a specialist in St. Cloud to have more testing done. As I walked back into my classroom and down the aisle, I realized that Mrs. Oatman must have explained to the class that I had a hearing problem. But I also realized that I wasn't too hard of hearing. One of the fourth graders whispered, "Now she's blind and deaf."

But no matter how much I didn't care for this third and fourth grade teacher, she inspired in me the desire to accomplish two things: to teach and write. After she doled out red pencils, each of us

Cindy in the schoolhouse at Santa Claus Town near Anoka

exchanged the spelling tests with the person in back of us. When I felt the power of that red lead go from my arm to my brain, I knew I wanted to become a teacher.

Mrs. Oatman also encouraged us to practice our penmanship by writing stories. During social studies, we read about Scotland and Wales and learned about the lives of young children in these countries. As a reinforcement to our assignment, we also watched a film. After she pulled down the screen from the top of the blackboard, she turned out the lights. We sat quietly listening to the low hum of the projector and the clickity clack of the film winding its way from one reel to the other. Soon we saw a a beam of light bounce on the screen and a black squiggly line. Once the film began, crumbling graying castles and lavender heather-covered moors enticed me to travel and write stories about other children and their homelands. I visualized myself being an ace reporter or feature writer for *LIFE*.

After surviving Mrs. Oatman, I graduated to the fifth grade classroom, upstairs, with the "big kids." Our teacher, who also did double duty as the principal, was Mrs. Weigand. With graying brown hair and hay-baling arms, she stood nearly six feet, or so all of us students thought. Everyone in our class could identify her mood just by observing her sitting at her desk as we walked into the classroom. If her hair had a few soft ringlets, she was in a good mood. If her hair was tight and curly, she was in a very bad mood and we'd better behave.

One morning before school, Bill tested our class theory. While he stood looking over the banister waiting for Mrs. Weigand to climb the steps, he churned up a wad of saliva and held it in his mouth. When she reached the half way mark, he forced a parachute of spit down on her tightly-coifed head. Her eyes became gray steel as she marched after Bill. With hands like iron grips, Mrs. Weigand grabbed Bill by his shirt collar when he tried to duck into the library. She hauled him into her office. When the bells rang, neither Mrs. Weigand nor Bill had returned to class. Students looked at the clock, then at each other. I took out my *Minnesota History* and re-read the assignment about the Sioux Uprising.

Postcards from the Old Man

When I entered the 7th grade in 1963, my childhood world changed. Adolescence began when I decided it was time to take a trip to Herberger's in St. Cloud, thirteen miles away, to buy my first training bra. I knew that I needed something on top even though Carol and Barb hadn't started wearing anything yet. Girls in the eighth grade wore these bandana-looking contraptions called training bras. Because I didn't know my correct size, and because I had a mother who didn't believe that I needed a bra yet, I asked the clerk for help. When I returned home, the Playtex box marked with 34C proved to my mother that, yes, her little girl had developed past the training period.

Another awakening happened one afternoon after school when Carol and I sat on our front steps. She told me about a book her mother had given her to read. She shocked me with images of elastic belts and scratchy pads that we would have to wear for much of our lives. She told me her mother called "it" either a curse or a blessing.

That night while I helped Mom with the dishes, I told her what Carol had told me. She blurted and mumbled excuses about my being too young to know such things. Two weekends later, while I visited my grandparents on their farm, I went into the bathroom. My first glance downward made me think I had a disease. As I sat on the commode, I remembered my discussion with Carol. Was this what her book had called "My friend"? I padded myself with Kleenix.

On the way home, I leaned forward in the car, whispering the news to my mother. When we got in the house, she walked to her bedroom and opened her closet. She handed me some emergency supplies but told me I would have to go Kniss's during my lunch hour to pick up more.

The next morning before school, I told Carol that I had a secret to tell her after lunch. During the lunch hour, I walked down to the grocery store. Beforehand, I hadn't thought about having to tell this elderly man behind the meat counter what I needed. My heart beat so hard I could feel it in my throat. I mumbled that my mother had called in an order for me. Mr. Kniss grabbed a blue and white box from the shelf in back of the butcher counter, quickly wrapped it in white paper, tied it with string, dropped it in a paper bag, and handed it to me. When I got back up the hill, Carol glanced in the bag. All she could say was "Geez."

I still loved Kurt in seventh grade, but so did Carol. He had grown tall like many of the boys, still had blonde hair--even though he tried to grease down his cowlick--and still had the adorable split in his two front teeth. Carol and I stared at him when he ran around the bases at recess. We ogled him when he walked into the room. We giggled and elbowed each other when he talked. When we stayed overnight at each other's houses, we shared secrets about him. When I saw him swimming at the Mill Pond, I noticed he had a farmer tan--white chest, but tanned neck and arms. I also shared with her that he wore a Sacred Heart medal on a chain around his neck. She told me she had seen him pinch his sister Darlene during Mass. Riding home from school, hiding low in the bus seat, we made up a song about our love for him.

It began, "I'm dreaming of a victory with Kurt," and could be sung to the tune of "White Christmas." Of course, no matter how many dreams we had about him, neither of us claimed victory.

I continued to dream about Kurt while listening to Ray Charles croon "I Can't Stop Loving You," but something happened that made me realize that a world existed outside of Clearwater. Returning to our desks following lunch break, my classmates and I faced a blackboard of questions. I don't remember what we were studying, but I do remember the silver radiators snapping and hissing, the phone ringing and invading my concentration, and our teacher, Mrs. Fobbe, announcing President Kennedy's assassination. I can also remember the smell of sweaty wool shirts from the boys' recent game of tag football and the faint odor of Bazooka Bubble Gum mingling with dusty oil from the recently mopped floor.

At recess time, no one asked to go outside to play jacks or Pom Pom Pullaway. Even Tim and Ernie, who were usually pulling pranks, sat as quietly as the rest of us listening to the radio. Most of us went home to televisions blaring black and white reruns of Walter Cronkite crying as he reported Kennedy's death. Unknowingly, we saw images that would be replayed for years to come: Aboard Air Force One, Lyndon Baines Johnson raising his right hand to take the oath of presidency while his wife Lady Bird stood on one side of him and Jaqueline Kennedy stood on the other side in her blood-stained dress; John-John saluting the flag-covered casket of his father as it traveled down Pennsylvania Avenue;

I began a slow awakening that cold day in November. Like our country, I too had to move on. In three short months, I screamed with thousands of teenagers when the Beatles invaded America, singing "I Want to Hold Your Hand" on the *Ed Sullivan Show*. For my eighth grade graduation, my mother allowed me to wear a bit of orange-glow lipstick and seamed nylons. Then, as I left Clearwater Elementary, like chalky hopscotch markings on a forgotten sidewalk, my childhood faded behind me.

PLEASANTLY SITUATED

"Good friends, good books,
and a sleepy conscience:
this is the ideal life."
Mark Twain, *Notebook*

WARNER LAKE

Long before hiking trails and picnic shelters, the Warner Lake I knew provided a perfect landscape for an imaginative child. Shortly after my sister Becky was born, our family moved to the Abeln farm, a half mile north of the Allen place. Here I enjoyed the sacraments of summer days.

Our yard provided a rich playground. White apple blossoms in the spring and red fruit in the fall canopied the front yard where my brother and I played tag. Pink blossoms and miniature fruit burst from the pear and plum trees in the back.

The yellow barn walls provided a prop for me to throw my softball near the peak of the roof and catch it with my brother's mitt. The front lawn sprawled out far enough for a game of softball. When friends or relatives came for a friendly meal-centered get-together, Dad (under

Pleasantly Situated

the duress of Mother who was tired of hearing kids ask when dinner was going to be ready) hollered "Batter Up!" as he stood on the mound and wound up for his slow pitch.

Tall pines bordered our yellow-stucco house. This secluded area formed a playhouse where I dragged my dolls, pinned a lace curtain to my head, clumped together a bridal bouquet of dandelions and clover, and marched to "Here Comes the Bride." Out front, I learned to ride a bike on the driveway that circled tiger lilies and bridal wreath.

Hardly a day went by that that I didn't wander down to Plum Creek that flowed out of Warner Lake. While wading in the shallow water below the rickety footbridge or building sandcastles with my sister, I watched muskrats swim to their dens. After reading the *Little House* books, I wondered if my Plum Creek, like Laura's, had dugouts. I wandered the bluffs, searching for depressions to feed my imagination.

Warner Lake filled my childhood days. Early weekend mornings, Dad and I grabbed cane poles and a can of worms. Loons laughed as we climbed into our boat, rowed to the middle of the lake, and waited for the sunfish to bite. After catching enough for lunch, we headed back to shore. Scaled, cleaned, rolled in cracker crumbs and fried, our catch provided our family crunchy nourishment.

When I became older, and could handle a boat myself, I climbed into the craft on sunny afternoons and cast afloat. Dangling my hand in the water and stroking the leathery lily pads, I read another adventure of Nancy, George, Bess, and Nick, and dog Togo in the latest Nancy Drew mystery I had taken out from the school library.

While daytime loomed with adventure, nighttime brought tranquility. As barn swallows swooped overhead, I gazed across the lake at the Camp Fire Girls' bonfire. Before heading to bed, I joined in with the girls from Camp Suima as they sang "Kumbaya."

Even though the smell of apple blossoms and the sound of camp songs have faded, my memories remain. And now, thanks to the

Postcards from the Old Man

Stearns County Park Department who preserved part of my childhood, I can go home anytime.

Pleasantly Situated

After we moved to Abelns, Carol's family "moved up" to the big house that we had just vacated. Only a half mile away from each other, we continued our visits and friendship.

Plum Creek

THE NEWLYWED GAME

Shaded by the evergreen trees,
a congregation of squirrels and bees
watched Cindy begin her bridal march
to her groom beneath the arch.

The gown of pearls and silk she'd worn
was Mom's blue dress with one sleeve torn.
Her veil of lace puffing in the wind
was a holey curtain, bobby-pinned.

With clumping heels, bouquet of clover,
she slowly marched beside old Rover
who was her father for the day
conscripted to give his girl away.

Cigar band ring; a quick embrace
but tears dripped down one childlike face.
The groom then stomped her feet and cried,
"next time I will be the bride."

Although we enjoyed our tranquil summers at the lake, we also experienced many typical summer brews—storms that often turned our world upside down.

Warner Lake

IN SEARCH OF OZ

    Steamy, mute afternoon—
        no singing meadowlarks singing
        no tapping crickets
        no clapping leaves.
        Silently, a wizard's cauldron brews.
        Across the pasture,
        a smoky black cape twirls toward the sky.
    Mother with diapered sister,
        and I with yipping mutt,
        crawl into the fruit-jarred tomb.
        We pause in musty dark
        when father closes the lid.
    A monkey screech of lawn chairs
        crashes against the house.
        Lions roar above our heads.
        Quaking cellar ceiling rages dust.
        Flickering candles illumine
        our ogling scarecrow eyes and gaping mouths.
    As quietness returns,
        we unearth ourselves to find:
        no yellow-brick road to follow,

Pleasantly Situated

    no ruby-red slippers to claim.

We sop through melted-witch puddles,
    sort through straw sticks, rusty tin,
    and window shards
    before stooping at the tipped wishing well
    to collect our copper hopes.

For my eighth birthday, Mom and Dad surprised me with the opportunity to begin piano lessons. Although I enjoyed the idea of becoming a concert pianist, my dream scaled down to dismal reality as I faced the keyboard for an hour every day.

THE PIANO LESSON

Mrs. Nelson drilled wrists-up—
baseball-cupped hands—
while cows eat glue buckets
and every good boy does fine.
As metronome clicked,
I clobbered black and white,
my own rendition of "Swan Lake,"
risking ruler slap for blending 1/4 and 1/2 notes.

Mrs. N reached over my shoulders.
With plump, freckled hands
smelling of rosewater,
she rolled up and down the octave,
tucking thumbs under,
illustrating how John Thompson
intended my nimble fingers
to dance a Fouetté across the 88.

Her protégé, I had turned tone-deaf the past week
to her instructions, "Practice. Practice. Practice!"
Instead, I pounded Beethovian Chopsticks
and twirled on the black, claw-footed stool,
my pony tail swatting my face.
I bowed before her spinet,
then clunked and tripped my way up the scales,
dreaming of Liberace and candlelight fame.

Pleasantly Situated

Summer days wouldn't have been complete without a jaunt down to the creek to play under the shade of the big trees.

PLUM CREEK PIRATES

At the creek,
    on a hot summer day
    I sit on the bank
    building a castle out of clay.
Only rain--or Donnie—can destroy.

Oh, here "he" comes
    on this hot summer day
    sneaking across the pasture
    to have his play.
"Cowboys or pirates? What'll it be?"

"Let's play pirates," I cunningly suggest.
    With a tree-branch sword,
    I lure him to the weathered-gray bridge.
    He threatens mutiny; I charge him in the chest.
"I'm Captain Hook.. Walk the plank."

Ha! There he goes
    on this hot summer day.
    Soggy and squishy, he's lost this naval war.
    No jolly roger,
    he mumbles and grumbles on his way,
dreaming and scheming how he'll even the score.

At the creek
    On a long, hot summer day,
    Alone . . . I smile at my castle out of clay.

Postcards from the Old Man

"PLUM CREEK" Todd Stupnik © 1987

In "What is Man?" Mark Twain says, "There is no act, large or small, fine or mean, which springs from any motive but the one—the necessity of appeasing and contenting one's own spirit." Children are often impetuous and impatient. I was no different. One summer, I received a lesson in responsibility, friendship, and ownership.

PONCHO

I remember when I first met Poncho. One spring afternoon as I headed home from school, I decided to take a short cut because I wanted to see our backyard bursting with bloom from white apple blossoms. As I walked along the leaf-packed path in back of the Campfire Girl's driveway, I heard a snap and a crunch. When I stopped and looked behind me, I saw a wagging brown tail to my right in the green of the woods. I crept closer and saw a small brown and black dog pawing for something under a fallen birch tree. The little critter looked up at me and barked. A bit frightened, I turned around and walked away as fast as I could. Soon the dog caught up to me, wagging its tail while following me all the way home.

My thirteen-year-old brother, Don, spotted my tag-a-long and me as we walked down the hill. He ran to meet us.

"Where did he come from?" he asked.

We both looked down at the fur ball on four legs. With his red tongue hanging out and his tail wagging, he looked up at the two of us.

I told Don about seeing the dog at the top of the hill and how he followed me home. My brother helped me put some left-over roast beef and water in white enamel bowls. We took our offerings to the dog who waited for us on the back steps. As he gobbled up the meat and lapped up the water, his tail wagged. Don and I talked about who his owners could be and if our folks would let us keep him.

Since Mom wasn't home, we went into the house, letting the dog follow us. Soon the mutt was running from room to room, sniffing in all the corners. He seemed to feel at home in the living room, curling up on the davenport and falling asleep.

I don't remember how we talked our folks into letting us keep the dog. But I do remember that the brown and black dog had the same coloring as the cow Dad slaughtered a few years before so we named him Poncho.

Poncho loved to chase after the baseball when Don and I played in the yard. We all got pretty good at throwing and retrieving sticks when we went down by the lake. But Poncho's playful personality came alive when he tried to catch carp in the fish trap by the creek. When Don and I said, "Sic'em, Poncho," the mutt seemed to bark happily. He looked like a flying squirrel as he aimed for the fish. With nose pointing in front, tail shooting backwards, front paws bending as back paws pushed off the rickety bridge, the dog sprang toward the water and landed with a splash. Don and I laughed at Poncho as he paddled toward shore, climbed the embankment, and shook water all over us.

Every morning either Don or I broke doggie burgers in the green plastic dog dish and filled up the coffee can with fresh water; Mom and Dad never had to remind us about feeding Poncho. Every evening before bedtime, we let him outside to do his business before he followed us upstairs to sleep on a brown rug in Don's room.

Then one morning after breakfast, I went outside and called "Poncho." I hollered for him a couple more times, but he didn't come running like usual. Don came in from riding his bike and said that the dog had run alongside him on the dirt road in front of house but then ran after something that caught his attention in the slough grass.

I stood on the front step and hollered for Poncho again, but he didn't come running. By suppertime, I began to worry. Had he been run over? Had he become lost? Dad and Mom didn't seem to be too concerned.

Pleasantly Situated

The next morning when I awoke, Poncho hadn't returned yet. Mom said she too wondered where he had gone. I filled his bowl and water can. I walked down to the shore and threw a stick into the lake. No Poncho. No Poncho by bedtime either.

Two days later, while Mom and I knelt planting radish seeds, Poncho bounded into the garden.

"Poncho!" I yelled as I hugged him. "Where have you been?"

He wagged his tail and licked my face.

Poncho hung around Don and me for two days. He joined in our games of catch. Then he took off again. This went on for three or four weeks.

"Can't we tie him up or keep him in the house so he won't wander off?" I asked Dad.

"How would you like to be tied up all the time and not able to explore around the country? Only city dogs have to be tied. Poncho needs freedom. Quit fretting. He can take care of himself."

I knew Dad was right, but I became more concerned when Mom said that we were going to Iowa to visit the cousins over the weekend. I always looked forward to seeing Kathy and Tom, but I worried that something would happen to Poncho while we were gone.

Since he had come home again, I begged my folks to let Poncho go with us. Mom said, "Absolutely not. You can't take a dog that is used to roaming the countryside two hundred miles in a car. Don't be so anxious; he'll be here when we get back."

No matter what she said, I worried. Poncho stayed away longer each time he left. I thought if he saw me leave, he'd think I wasn't coming back and he'd take off for good.

Postcards from the Old Man

I came up with a secret plan. Saturday morning, before we left, I smuggled Poncho into the cellar. I put several big bowls of water and dog food in with him. Mom had Don and Dad so busy hauling suitcases and boxes of gifts to the car that they didn't pay any attention to me. Finally, Dad hollered that it was time to go.

"Just be good," I ordered Poncho. "We'll be back in three days." I tried not to think of how lonely or trapped he would be while we were gone. At least I felt relieved that he would be here when we got back.

We had a great time in Iowa. Don, Kathy, Tom, and I had always been close because we were the oldest of all the cousins. Aunt Arlene, Mom's sister, came up with the idea of seeing who could eat the most pancakes. Don won but that was because he was the oldest and the biggest of the four of us.

Kathy decided we should put on a circus show on the front porch. Of course, both sets of folks had to be captive audiences. I was the barker and announced all the acts. First, Tom walked the tight rope (teeter totter). Then Don, in Uncle Ernie's blue terry bathrobe, played Zoroff the Magician while Kathy became Zita his assistant. Wearing her black swimming suit, she disappeared behind a green army blanket. Next Tom rode his bike in circles without using his hands and feet like our Grandpa Johnson had taught him. While Tom rode, Kathy twirled her baton, throwing it up in the air and catching it before twirling it around her waist. I attempted to juggle apples and oranges, but most of them landed on the grass. In the final act, Don led Kathy and Tom's dog Barnie by his chain, pretending he was an elephant.

I had so much fun that I forgot about Poncho until we started back for home. Squeezed in the back seat with my brother and a mass of hand-me-down clothes and comic books, I began to think that Mom and Dad might be a little surprised to see Poncho when I let him out of the house.

Pleasantly Situated

When we pulled in the driveway, Mom told Don and me to take a suitcase and a box so Dad wouldn't have to haul it all by himself. Dad opened the front door as we all stood behind him waiting to enter the house.

"Phewy!" he said.

The rest of us followed in after Dad. "E-yuck!" Don and I howled. As we started to sniff, we realized the smell became worse in the living room, especially near the davenport. Dad tipped it on its end. An ugly fur ball—a dead rat—lay under the corner.

I heard a whimper. All of a sudden, I remembered Poncho. I ran to the cellar door. As soon as I opened it, the dog limped out. I looked down at his paw and saw blood. Poncho barked. I tried to pick up the dog's leg, but he growled at me.

"What is going on?" Dad asked when he came out to the kitchen to get the broom and dustpan.

For an instant I tried to think of something to say. Dad stood two feet from Poncho and me. There was no way to hide the truth.

"I didn't want Poncho to run away again. I put him downstairs before we went to Iowa. Now something is wrong with him. He almost bit me."

Dad stooped over and looked at Poncho. I saw scratches and dried blood all over the dog's face. Dad pushed me into the living room with the rest of the family. I heard the back door slam and Poncho's whine.

After a few minutes, Dad came back in the house and told Mom to call a vet. "That rat got into a fight with the dog. The rat might have been rabid," he told her while Don and I listened.

"What is rabid?" I whispered to Don.

"Don't you remember *Old Yeller*?"

I remembered what happened to that dog. I knew that Dad might have to shoot Poncho if he had rabies. I felt guilty about locking him in the cellar.

After Mom hung up the phone, she told Dad that Poncho needed to be tied up away from all us for two weeks. We were to keep an eye on the dog to see if he attempted to snap or bite at one of us, became extremely thirsty, or started foaming at the mouth, all signs of the disease.

Two weeks dragged on forever. Mom and Dad grounded me. I couldn't visit Carol and I couldn't talk on the phone.

"So you won't forget what it is like to not be able to run and play like Poncho," Mom said.

Every day, after Dad delivered Poncho's food and water, I asked if the dog were showing any symptoms. Dad always said, "Not yet."

I couldn't concentrate well in school. I tossed in bed at night because I kept seeing Poncho chained up on the barn and Dad shooting him.

Don was angry too. "How could you be so dumb?"

Finally the vet came to check on Poncho. He and Dad went into the barn and closed the door behind them. About five minutes later Poncho ran out and streaked across the pasture.

I shouted, "Poncho, come back here." But he kept running.

I felt even more miserable. "He'll never come back now," I told Carol. "He doesn't know why I locked him in the cellar nor why Dad locked him in the barn."

Pleasantly Situated

Don and I couldn't throw sticks into the water for Poncho to fetch. The dog didn't run down the driveway to meet us when we came home after school.

One Saturday Mom asked me to go visit Mrs. Jacobs, an elderly woman who lived on a farm on the road to St. Augusta. When we pulled into her yard, I looked in the porch and saw Mrs. Jacobs sitting in a wicker rocking chair with a brown and black dog sitting on the floor by her feet.

"Poncho?"

The small brown bundle of fur scampered down the steps, barking all the way.

"Buster, come back here. Stop that barking."

As I opened the back door, he jumped on me, licking my hands and face.

"Did you call him Buster?" I asked Mrs. Jacobs.

"Did you call him Poncho?" Mrs. Jacobs asked me.

All of us talked at once. Poncho-Buster ran back and forth, wagging his tail, jumping, barking, and licking all of us as we patted his head and back.

Mrs. Jacobs said that her son gave Buster to her for Christmas a year before. "He was worried about me being alone since Mr. Jacobs passed on. But over the past few months he has been taking off for a few days at a time. This last time he was gone for over two weeks and I thought he was dead."

Mom and I both started to say that Poncho had been at our house. I told Mrs. Jacobs about finding him in the woods behind our house as I was going to school. Mom told her about our trip to Iowa and the rabies scare. She never mentioned my locking the dog in the basement. "We had no idea he was your dog."

We pieced the puzzle together. Poncho-Buster had been living with Mrs. Jacobs and us at the same time.

Because he belonged to her, I knew that I couldn't keep him, no matter how much I loved him. But I still asked, "Can I please come visit him sometimes?"

Mrs. Jacobs laughed. "Of course. And he can come visit you, too. I think Buster decided that he wanted to play with children at times. But he likes coming home too. Why don't we just let him keep commuting?"

The more we thought about it, the more we liked the idea. Any dog that would run back and forth five miles to see all of us must like us. I learned an important lesson that day. In a way, we all owned Buster-Poncho. In another way, none of us did. Poncho was our friend. But friends must be free to have other friends.

In the weeks ahead, when Don and I got home from school, Poncho was often waiting for us, with his tail wagging. Sometimes, on weekends, we saw him racing for our farm, ready to catch a fish in mid air or chase a stick. Then Poncho wagged his tail, as if to say goodbye, and Buster headed for home.

Pleasantly Situated

"For all the talk you hear about knowledge being such a wonderful thing, instinct is worth forty of it for real unerringness.
-- Mark Twain, *Tom Sawyer Abroad* --

A LITTLE KNOWLEDGE

My folks bought my first bike from Monkey Wards. A green Hawthorne, with a chrome, streamlined book rack leaned against the garage door waiting for me to find it on my eighth birthday in May. Dad said that as soon as we ate breakfast, he'd give me my first riding lesson. After a few pushes and instructions from him, as well as a bit of determination on my part, I learned that a little knowledge can be a dangerous thing.

After Dad tightened the last bolt on my new bike, he began to teach me to ride. While he firmly grasped the handlebars, I hopped on the green vinyl seat. By placing both feet on the pedals, I attempted my first balancing routine. Even though Dad guided me protectively by holding on to the front and chrome back fender, I felt unsure of myself as I wobbled back and forth. After a moment or two, I gained some composure and tried to hold the bike still without tipping over. While I pedaled, Dad led me around the circle-driveway by pulling me by the handlebars. With his patience and my practice, we worked together as a team. Unfortunately, because of my lack of confidence, when he took his hands off the handlebars, I became frightened and tipped over. After an hour, Dad said that I had ridden enough for one day. I put the bike in the garage, carefully wiping the imagined dust from it before going swimming.

Thank goodness I was stubborn and determined because the next morning after Dad went to work, I faced the Hawthorne alone and told it that I was going to be its master. I pushed up the kickstand and straddled the bike. Finally, I braved sitting on the seat while placing my feet on the pedals. I rocked back and forth before tipping over and pulling the bike on top of me. Again, while I clenched my teeth, I mounted the bike and held my balance for a few seconds before beginning the rock-and-roll motion. For some time I tried gaining coordination. I was like a ballerina trying to balance on her toes, only I tried to balance on bike pedals. I got a little more nerve and pushed myself forward. My confidence began to build as I went a few feet before losing control. Soon I was circling the driveway with the wind blowing back my hair.

After a week of driving in circles, I told my folks that I was ready to ride to my friend Carol's, a half-mile away. I pumped the pedals fast to get up the sandy hill between our houses. Once I arrived at the top, I biked easily the rest of the way to her house.

For awhile I played tag and teased Carol's brothers, but the time came when I had to head home. I loved the feeling of freedom that my new green bike gave me. Nearing the bottom of the hill, I picked up speed to reach the top, which I did with ease. As I headed downwards, I felt like a daredevil because of my uncontrolled speed. About half way to my driveway, I realized that I was going too fast. It didn't take me long to realize that Dad had neglected to teach me one small detail—how and when to apply the brakes when riding down a hill. Down and down I rode, occasionally swerving in the thick sand. My heart pounded as I screamed, but I managed to stay on that bucking bronco of a bike. As I steered toward the direction of the driveway, I went head over bike, slamming into the wooden post that held our black mailbox.

My biking days came to a sudden halt for about two weeks while I recuperated from an infected kneecap and a bad disposition. During that time, I learned one thing about my biking incident: a *little* knowledge can be a dangerous thing.

Pleasantly Situated

I learned the lesson about riding down a sandy hill without using my brakes, but sometime later, I learned a more important lesson.

THE CYCLE

Your calloused, sausage-fingers gripped
back chrome fender,
guiding my green Hawthorne
while I jiggled and you ran
down gravel driveway
and up grassy trails.

Years later, as I clutched
the banana seat of my son's Huffy,
sprinting as he pedaled left and right
over swollen and cracked sidewalks,
I saw your hand, Dad,
like mine,
lift after the first push.

Postcards from the Old Man

Winters at the lake held their own charm. Except for the path the landlord's tractor made for us from the road to our house, snow mounds covered the yard. Probably because I was older, Christmas seasons took on a different dimension here as well.

YES, VIRGINIA

Navy blue, crystally winter's night.
Glittering sifted snow, icing topped lake,
evergreens muffed in white. I plodded
as Becky pulled me down the glossy road.

A bundle of blue, she sometimes followed,
sometimes led, sometimes jumped over my feet
as she chattered about baby dolls, Santa's snack—
star-shaped cookies, his tummy and our chimney.

Late autumn's whispered secret unmasked the man.
A grown up woman of ten, I played my part
for my younger sister that Christmas Eve,
although I no longer believed.

Carolers sang, "...won't you guide my sleigh tonight?"
I grumbled, "It's time to go home."
As I turned, my eye caught a wink of light
dashing across the blue-black sky.

Becky and I tumbled through pockets of snow.
The yard glowed—lit house and trees.
I blinked.
Who hunched in the shadows?

Mom, traditionally dressed in pink flannel gown,
pulled off our coats and pushed us into the living room.
Becky ran to a diapered doll and teddy bear.
I gazed at a white-veiled Barbie,
Betty Crocker Bake Set, white fur-topped boots.

Pleasantly Situated

On the floor lay the empty green 7UP bottle
and a plate of cookie crumbs.
I ran to the window. Cupped my hands around my eyes.
No reindeer, no sleigh.

And on that navy blue, crystally winter's night,
I decided to believe for one more year.

SMOKE AND GOSSIP

Dick's Lunch

"Do not tell fish stories
where the people know you;
but particularly,
don't tell them where they know the fish."
-- Mark Twain, *More Maxims of Mark Twain* --

Talking Over the Situation

> "There is no act, large or small, fine or mean, which springs from any motive but the one—the necessity of appeasing and contenting one's own spirit."
> --Mark Twain, "What Is Man?"--

In the early 60s, Mother and her friend Alvina sat around the kitchen table, coffee cups in hand, chatting about kids, husbands, gardens, and the lack of a decent restaurant in Clearwater. Mom said she heard that the owner of Dick's Lunch, a local diner-type café, seriously considered leasing out his building. The two of them mulled over the diner's possibilities. Alvina said she could whip up the desserts; people often called on her to decorate birthday and wedding cakes. Mom said she could offer the town's lunch crew a hardy meat and potatoes meal during the noon hour.

When Alvina left their little coffee klatch, she didn't give their entrepreneurship venture much consideration. In fact, later in the week, when Mom and she were talking again, she fessed up that she didn't feel she could leave her regular paying job as a cook at Woolworth's in St. Cloud. Mom understood; money was often tight in both households and running this little restaurant was a gamble she wasn't sure she wanted to tackle either.

But the more Mom thought about it, the more she wanted to try her hand at this gastronomical affair. She called Clyde Powers, the owner of the little building on top of the hill in Clearwater, and set up an appointment to talk with him. After looking over the diner, Mom knew that the small edifice could never become a five-star restaurant. But she also had the foresight to know that it was situated in a great location for Clearwater, right off 152 at the edge of town. Semis and cars stopped to fill their gas tanks and the Greyhound stopped to drop off and pick up passengers. Mom decided to go it alone. With the signing of the rental papers, our family's lives began to revolve around this little diner.

Smoke and Gossip

Every morning before dawn, Dad took Mother and her gray metal cash box into town so she could open the restaurant. As soon as he grabbed a quick cup of coffee, he headed off to his own job at the foundry in St. Cloud.

In the afternoon, the whole family met back there to eat supper and help Mom close up. Becky was usually saddled up on one of the green plastic and chrome stools when I got home from elementary school. Don came home from high school to help with the late afternoon crowd, which was often a group of his own friends who needed a quick fill up of crispy fries, chocolate malts, or Cokes. In the early evening, Dad stopped at home to bathe before heading into town to eat and get us all home for the evening. This little building became our new home where we celebrated birthdays and holidays, while soaking up some local color.

Postcards from the Old Man

HOSPITALITY RECEIVED

**"There are few stories that have anything superlatively good in them except the idea—and that is always bettered by transplanting."
-- Mark Twain, "Letter to William Dean Howells, 1876" --**

The village diner, hometown eatery, has become almost a thing of the past as it gives way to Country Kitchens, Happy Chefs, and Perkins. Long before Burger King came to town, my mother's café, Dick's Lunch, catered to the town citizens' needs to eat a nourishing meal and socialize.

With its white false front, the small square edifice sat right off old highway 152. For a number of years, the building watched over the western prairie all by itself. But in the 50's and 60's, the construction of a Texaco station, owned by Art Maness, and barbershop, operated by Tom McDonald, joined with Dick's Lunch to make up Clearwater's version of a mini-mall.

When my mom, Winnie, took over the café, busy farmers, pulling in to get a dollar's worth of gas at the green and white filling station, ran over to to get an ice cream cone for their ride home. Teens who stopped at the station to check the oil in their hot rods clambered up the steps to get a Coke. After plopping fifteen cents on the counter, they hopped back in their souped-up cars and squealed their tires, spraying dust squalls before they continued cruising the town.

Even though Mom's little restaurant may never have been part of the world's top echelon of eating establishments, her cuisine never suffered. Customers saddled up to one of the green stools that surrounded the L-shaped counter to order one of her specialties. Winnie's menu included typical short orders like BLT's, grilled cheese, and a soup of the day like beefy vegetable or chicken noodle. With her friend Joyce, who often showed up in the morning carrying a round dishpan heaping with glazed donuts she had made in the wee hours of the morning, Mom prepared noon meals for those who worked at the different town businesses like the T&O Plastic Plant and Tri-County Lumber. They scooped up generous helpings of golden brown pork chops and buttery mashed potatoes, baked ham and creamy scalloped potatoes, New England boiled dinner, and, of course, Mom's specialty, hot beef sandwiches smothered in rich brown gravy. A triangle of hot apple or sugary, lattice-covered cherry pies made these noon meals complete.

Like many customers, I satisfied my pre-teen diet with one of Mom's tasty hamburgers. When the patty cooked through on the grill, she tossed the top and bottom of the buns under the broiler for a few seconds. From the momentary contact of the greasy spatula, the buns turned a crusty brown. After dousing the beef with plenty of ketchup, mustard, and a layer of thinly sliced pickles, one of her creamy chocolate malts made all this go down better.

Although the food was filling and tasty, many people congregated at Winnie's to gobble up on town news. The café became the town meeting hall, the church basement, and the town square. Around the L-shaped counter, her patrons sipped on their bottomless cups of coffee while they nominated mayors, hired and often fired reverends, and gossiped about unwed mothers.

George Henson, a local historian who lived through many of the town's changes and had the local jail still sitting on his property, frequented Mother's eatery. Tall, gray-haired, and handsome in his 70's, George drove up almost every afternoon for a bite to eat.

Not only did George like to gab, but in his own right, he created gossip around town just by his driving. In the early 1900's, during Clearwater's glory days, George worked as a drayman. With whip in hand to steer his team of horses, he controlled the road. A man about his business, George delivered goods from ferry or depot to the grocery stores or the post office. If shoppers and dalliers didn't want to be sprayed with dust or mud, they stayed clear of him as he pushed his horses to keep on schedule.

Unfortunately, once automobiles took over the roads, George had a hard time adopting Minnesota's driving regulations and sharing the road. When he climbed behind the steering wheel of his 1948, silver-gray Ford coupe, he seldom used the car's turn signals or obeyed the one hundred yard rule (if he even knew about it to begin with). Instead, when George neared his turn, he slammed on his brakes, indicating he intended to turn NOW, and rotated his car where he aimed it. If he wanted to go right, he veered wide into the oncoming lane. If he wanted to go left, his wheels usually hooked the curb or sidewalk. He also paid little or no attention to stop or yield signs because he figured he still had dominion on the streets.

But George's most dangerous driving infractions occurred because he had no concept of "keep right." One time in particular, as George headed up the Blacksmith's Hill (named for the blacksmith shop at the bottom of the hill on Main Street), the elderly man had a close call with an approaching car. As usual, George had been driving in the middle of the street. When the other driver started to descend the hill, he didn't see the elderly man's vehicle until he was about twenty-five feet away. After the stranger honked a couple times, he swerved to the right to get out of George's way, missing him by inches.

Mom could tell that George was agitated when he sat down at the counter. She asked if he were all right because she noticed he was shaking. Once he calmed down, he told his side of the story. George said that a stranger in town had "aimed his car right at me" when they met on the hill. He called the man in the other car a "black sinner," which was his expression for anyone he didn't like or who he thought had done him wrong. Of course, Mom and almost everyone else who heard his story knew that, more than likely, George had been the cause of the near accident. The elderly citizen could never get it through his head that the streets were now used for two-way traffic.

Regulars for late lunches or early suppers, George and his steady girlfriend, Myrtle Johnson, resembled Laurel and Hardy—willowy George and plump Myrtle. Well-known in town for giving kids piano lessons, Myrtle took it upon herself to give every young man recruited into the military a Bible. Although George and Myrtle never formalized their relationship with marriage, they went together to town picnics, church socials, Sunday afternoon drives, and of course, noon lunches at our café. Their relationship created quite a bit of jealously for another town citizen, Emma Michael. All three individuals had lost their spouses years before. And while Emma had always been reserved, when she made up her mind she wanted George, she attempted to track her man. Often, she called Mother in the afternoon asking whether George and Myrtle had shown up for lunch yet. Mother knew she couldn't lie and told her that the two had been in the café, even though she knew that this information would hurt Emma. According to Mother, Emma hesitated before saying thank you and hanging up. George knew that Emma was interested in him, but he had set his cap on Myrtle.

On lazy Friday afternoons, the couple lingered at the counter, long after the lunch crowd had been fed and the kitchen had been cleaned to gab with Joyce, Mother, and other customers about early Clearwater. Often they still sat there, with my sister plopped between them on a stool, when I arrived from the brown, two-story school building a couple blocks away.

While Myrtle had received her news from the party line, George had picked up the latest while playing checkers at Clearwater Coal and Feed. Although at times the two interrupted one another to argue over the other's historical recollections, they agreed on one topic—Clearwater's heyday had passed. Their spirited conversations that brought life to the town's past and its early citizens fed this young girl's imagination.

Winnie and Becky outside Dick's Lunch

Postcards from the Old Man

LEGENDS AND SCENERY

**"Truth is stranger than fiction, but it is because Fiction is obliged to stick to possibilities; Truth isn't."
-- Mark Twain, *Following the Equator* --**

Once the last person from the regular lunch crowd paid his or her check, Mom took away Myrtle's and George's dirty lunch plates and brought them either dessert plates of lemon-yellow sugar cookies or slices of apple pie, one with a slab of orange cheese melted on top for George and the other with a dollop of vanilla ice cream for Myrtle.

Becky Frank about 1962 at Dick's Lunch

After Mom refilled their coffee, she poured herself a mug, popped open an Orange Nesbitts for Becky, and sat down on a stool to take five. Often, as I opened the back door after the 3:15 dismissal from school, I found the quartet huddled around the counter. The dusty shaft of afternoon sun kindled their stories about early Clearwater.

According to George, back in 1855, two men, Asa White and Alonzo Boyington, paddled up the Mississippi and dropped anchor by the outlet of the Clearwater River. He said that the two men named the grassy landing that both rivers shared El Dorado.

Sometime later, another voyager, Simon Stevens, brother of Colonel John Stevens, Minneapolis' founder, also paddled north to

Smoke and Gossip

where the Clearwater River empties into the Mississippi. While White and Boyington had left the area to buy supplies, Stevens and his fellow travelers had also traveled up the Mississippi. They stopped at the same natural, grassy landing but named it Clearwater. When the two groups finally met, a small skirmish broke out when each claimed it had been first to set foot on the future town site. Someone calmly diffused the situation before too much blood was shed. Stevens' choice won and the Clearwater area began to fill up with men looking for homestead land or business opportunities.

As Myrtle nibbled on her dessert, she said that her parents had told her that the early river village had hopped with activity. Two-story hotels, general stores, jewelry stores, drugstores, blacksmith shops, millinery shops, livery stables, grain elevators, and paper and flour mills made the town a busy commercial center. In addition, ferries crossed east and west over the river, and steamships, like the *H.B. Bassett,* came up from St. Paul, hauling cargo and passengers to the village shores. I thought of downtown's old buildings where shingles had blown off roofs and black asphalt had been torn from the sidings and found it hard to believe that at one time our slumbering village had been such a busy metropolis.

Wannigan on the Mississippi River at Clearwater sometime before 1900

Then George reminded everyone about Clearwater's lost opportunity. Apparently, representatives from the Burbank Stage Company out of St. Paul met with a few town fathers to tell them of their plan to build a road from the Mississippi River landing at Clearwater to Cold Spring. They said they needed land for livery stables, barns, and warehouses in order to care for and house livestock and supplies for their Red River journeys to the northern towns of Moorhead, Fargo, Grand Forks, and even further into Canada. They said that if Clearwater became the company's hub, their association would mean profits--the company would profit by cutting fifteen miles from its original route through St. Cloud, and Clearwater would profit by the tradesmen's patronage of local hotels and mills.

At this point in his conversation, George usually started wagging his finger about the lack of foresight by town's movers and shakers. By-sakes, he'd say, (another George-ism), they flat out refused the offer because they feared the developers would tear up some of the county's richest farming land. Because of the founders' prudence, Clearwater's loss became St. Cloud's gain. George went on to say that many old-timers believed that Clearwater could have become a large city like St. Cloud.

George or Myrtle usually brought up the fact that only a few of the original town buildings remained; the ones they talked about I recognized as relics from the past. The small Westcott building looked larger than it was because of its false front and low hanging

City Hall on the left and Westcott building in the middle

windows on each side of the front door. Mom said that the building, owned by the Westcott family, had been a small café and sat by the railroad tracks. Many passengers stopped here for refreshments before reboarding the train and heading to their final destinations.

She also said that when the Lyons family bought the building, they moved it closer to their home on the north end of Main Street where it became a small general store. Unfortunately, after awhile, this building, like many others in town, began to suffer neglect. A few of the historically-unconcerned had used the building to store the bell for the old city hall, as well as plows and shovels for street maintenance, which ruined the floor. In addition, the ceiling caved in and the back lean-to began to collapse.

Many times I had walked on the sidewalk by the dilapidated edifice, gazed in one of the side windows, and dreamed of turning the building into an ice cream parlor. I visualized people sitting at the parlor tables or at the counter being served by a white-aproned soda jerk.

The Masonic Lodge, upper right side, on the corner of Main and Oak

The Masonic Lodge, another remnant, saw plenty of activity for a number of years. The original structure was built in 1873, mainly as a meeting place for the Masonic Lodge members. When a fire destroyed the building in July, 1888, a new one was built by January, 1889. Over the years, the two-story edifice with meeting hall on the top floor and room for two stores on the bottom housed the Masons and Eastern Star, a number of general stores, and a beer hall. At times, local businesses, including Kloeppner's Appliance and T & O Plastics, stored appliances and inventory here, as well.

As Mom's little covey talked, I remembered going to one of Herman Kloeppner's appliance auctions downstairs of the lodge with my folks. We sat on brown folding chairs and watched men roll appliances to the center stage. An auctioneer opened washing machine covers and stove and refrigerator doors. He took out burners and shelves. He said "GE stands behind its appliances" and "quality is always first." Then the man rolled his tongue with a lingo that I had never heard before. Each time an individual's hand shot up with what looked like a popscicle stick with numbers written with red crayon on a white circle, the auctioneer raised the price of the appliance. Once it turned quiet for a bit, the auctioneer said, "SOLD!"

Then Mr. Kloeppner and a teenage girl came to the center stage with a bucket. He told the audience that they were going to draw for one of the door prizes. To locate the winning number, the audience was supposed to look under the seat of the chair where the winning number was taped. After stirring up the folded slips of paper with her hand, the girl pulled one out. Mr. Kloeppner took it from her and read the number. People scrambled to tip their chairs to see if they'd won a prize. One by one, the audience sat back down on their chairs, disappointed they hadn't won anything. Dad helped me with my chair. We were both surprised to find that a number was taped to the bottom of my seat. He pulled off the slip and raised my arm, indicating I was the winner. That day I proudly took home a round, white clock that Mom proudly hung over the refrigerator. Sooner after this, the temple, another rare vestige of the past, began to sponsor fewer and fewer events, and like the Westcott building, the two-story, yellow sandstone structure began to stare vacantly at passersby.

However important these buildings were, in my eyes, the most impressive village building stood next to the school. Whenever the after-lunch

Congregational Church, artist Billy Auwater

Smoke and Gossip

crowd's conversation got around to the Sioux Uprising of 1862, I knew that they'd eventually get around to talking about the Congregational Church. While many stories about the town's early settlement held my interest, the story about the white-sided structure that loomed next to the Clearwater Elementary School fascinated me the most. Whether I stood against the building trying to balance myself on stilts or threw marbles against the school's outer walls, my gaze eventually drifted beyond the lilac bushes and over to the church.

I thought about the stories George, Myrtle, and Mom shared about the building's early days when it was used as a fort. Mom said that because so many men had volunteered to serve in the Civil War, Minnesotans were left unprotected from raiding Indians. Apparently, after the Dustin family came under attack in southern Wright County, killing all but two, many people fled their farms to take refuge in the nearest towns where stockades had been built.

After hearing about the disaster, Clearwater citizens decided they needed to protect themselves. Believing the Congregational Church on the hill provided them the best safety because it was new and offered an excellent view of the western prairie as well as the Mississippi, they ordered the saw mill located on the Clearwater River to cut enough timber to fortify the church. In addition, they directed them to drill rifle notches at the tops of the planks. The men then overlapped planks on the inside and built a stockade around the outside. As I sat listening to the trio's stories, I imagined a scenerio where the town came under attack. I saw men, wearing long–sleeved gray shirts tucked into dark wool trousers held up with suspenders. With their guns posed in the notches, the men stood guard to defend their families and the rest of the town. Women, dressed in gingham and wearing poke bonnets, huddled with their children in the church.

Even though the attack never came, the tunnel below the church became legend. Besides building the fortress, insightful Clearwaterites dug a three-foot crawl space from the church's basement to the river's edge where those escaping could board the ferry and be transported to safety. All precautions were taken, but thankfully, no attack occurred. Sometime later, when all fear had subsided, someone boarded up the unused passageway, allowing prairie grass to cover up the opening and leaving the tunnel's history to curiosity seekers and storytellers.

While some of the early buildings had interesting histories, I liked listening to the flesh and blood stories the most. I especially enjoyed the tales George or Myrtle told about some of the early settlers. I felt Abigail Camp epitomized the true pioneer spirit. After she became a widow at a very early age, she traveled from out east—Vermont, George thought—to become a housekeeper for a hotel built by Stevens and a few others.

Abigail Camp

At this point, Myrtle added that in 1855, Mrs. Camp, supposedly the first woman in Wright County, came up the Mississippi on a steamboat one morning. She said the story goes that sometime that evening, after the saloon keeper spread a tavern door across sawhorses, Mrs. Camp served her first meal of salt pork and fried potatoes to hotel guests.

Thomas Porter

By this time, someone around the lunch counter usually brought up the fact that about a year after her arrival in Clearwater, Abigail Camp married Thomas Porter, another early settler. Mom added that Thomas came from Pennsylvania in 1855 and opened a tavern on the other side of the river. George said that he was always told that the man built his entire house from the lumber that drifted down the Mississippi. As the group continued to talk about Thomas Porter and his accomplishments, I gathered that he was an important wheeler and dealer because someone commented that he became state representative back in the 1880's.

The lunch crowd's gab often took them to the Phillips family and to the illustrious Jenny, or Jane to her family. I had seen many pictures of her. Dressed in a long skirt and white blouse, sporting old-fashioned wire-rimmed spectacles, she wore curly bangs and twirled the rest of her hair in a bun. I romanticized about the stories I had heard about her love for a man she couldn't marry and her resistance to marrying anyone else.

Jenny Phillips

Jane had become a career girl, and I admired her for this. She went to school to learn pharmacy, and when her father retired as the town pharmacist, she took over Phillips Drugstore that also housed the post office. I imagined Jane wearing a white pharmacist smock, bending over a counter crushing medicines in a mortar and pestle, and greeting town citizens as they came in for their morning mail.

But, while I enjoyed sitting on a stool sipping Coke from a straw and listening to the adults' conversations about the early citizens, those long-dead were merely actors on a stage. Mostly, I liked hearing about those historic characters, who, still living, linked Clearwater to its past.

Jeannette Whittemore was one such person. Myrtle told us that Mrs. Whittemore had once been a teacher for Clearwater back in the early 1900s and her husband owned Whittemore Bank and Insurance Agency. I knew her. For a fall project, we MYFers chose a Saturday to help the elderly. We offered to rake lawns, wash windows, and clean their houses. I worked for Mrs. Whittemore.

When she opened the back door after I knocked, her appearance surprised me. Instead of a shriveled up and bent over elderly lady, she stood tall and straight, resembling the pictures I had seen of her standing with her students on the school's front steps. From head to foot, her wardrobe and appearance portrayed an earlier period though. She wore a long black dress with a white lace collar. Her gray hair flowed back from her forehead in tight wavelets that merged into a twirled bun at the crown of her head from which I expected to see a pencil. As she walked, I noticed she sported black, high-buttoned shoes.

Mom interrupted my thoughts when she said that both Jeanette Whittemore and Lucy Murray, another elderly citizen, always wore their fox furs wrapped around their necks and used canes when they went for leisurely walks downtown. While Mrs. Whittemore leaned on hers, seemingly dependent upon its usefulness for keeping her gait steady, Lucy usually hid hers at the edge of Main Street in Heaton's lilac bushes because she had too much pride to let others see her using it.

At the time I was growing up, Maude, daughter of Abigail Camp and Thomas Porter, was Clearwater's most important link to the past. Mom reminded all of us sitting around the lunch counter that the town's centenarian and Governor Freeman dedicated the new bridge that spanned the Mississippi back in the early 60s. The *St. Cloud Times* reported the story and displayed a wonderful picture of the two people. The picture showed Maude shorter than I remembered, probably because she was so stooped, and shaking the governor's hand while holding onto her hat because it was so windy.

The frail woman in the picture wasn't the Maude Porter I had known. I remembered a tall, thin woman who I believed never kept up with the times. She and some of her contemporaries like Jeannette Whittemore and Lucy Murray still wore their long hems and black high-top shoes in the early 1960s. As the elderly lunch crowd talked about Maude's life in town, I thought of her house that had turned brown with age. A couple of oaks shaded the roof and lilac bushes covered the windows, producing long scary shadows during the day and night. If Maude had electricity, she used it sparingly. Seldom, day or night, did I see a light on. Of course, since Maude was over one

Maude Porter's calling card

hundred when she finally went to a nursing home, she went to bed early, avoiding the need for lights. In fact, up to the time she moved away, she still used the chamber pot and the privy that tilted in her back yard.

No matter if she still lived in antiquity, Maude Porter was a rarity. Mom reminded us that for Clearwater's Centennial, Maude rode in a Model A with banners on both sides of the car that read "Women's Temperance Society." I remembered I had heard her speak her mind about the "younger generation" at the Old-Timers picnic in Upper Park. She said "they don't have enough to do nowadays." She went on to say, "Now in my day, boys and girls who lived in town went to school all day, had chores like emptying slop pails, washing dishes, and taking in the laundry from the clotheslines." In addition to helping around their homes, "they often worked out of their homes sweeping out the grocery store, helping neighbor women with their children, or unloading cartons down at the depot." (Maude's charge always contradicted George's comments that she never worked out of the home until she was older. In fact, her parents spoiled their only child and seldom made her lift a finger to help them with the household chores. George often laughed when he added that years later, she had a habit of showing up at friends' homes at suppertime so she wouldn't have to cook for herself.) As my generation listened to her speak at the picnics, no one took this elderly woman's comments too seriously because we figured she just wasn't with it anymore; times had changed. We lived in a new world of hotrods, baseball games, hoola-hoops, and the Twist.

Maude Porter in 1962 sitting on her front porch on Main Street when she was 100

Mom said that when Maude fell and broke her hip after she turned one hundred, she started to fail. When a few of her closest friends decided that it was time for her to sell her place and enter a nursing home, they held an auction.

George said that he couldn't remember ever seeing the town streets so full of cars. Myrtle remembered how packed Maude's yard was with sightseers meandering around trying to get a glimpse of all the antique dressers, chairs, and beds.

Mom asked if anyone remembered how much the dealers paid for that large walnut chifforobe that her father Thomas had sent for from out east after he'd been here awhile. No one seemed to remember, but they all agreed that the antique dealers outbid all the locals for most of Maude's belongings.

As they continued to talk of Maude's furniture, I daydreamed about that day. I remembered seeing the car-lined streets, the multitude of people with familiar and not so familiar faces, and backs of people carrying chairs, cardboard boxes full of dishes, and books to take back to their cars. I remembered circles of people standing around a hay wagon as the auctioneer pleaded "*Gimmemmme gimme a bidddd.*"

My friend Carol had come from the country to partake in the festivities. We wandered around Maude's yard, rummaging through a few boxes filled with glassware and lard cans looking for souvenirs we could afford to buy.

We both tiptoed to a side window, cupped our hands, and peeked in. I recognized Mrs. Jorgenson and Mrs. Sanders standing around an old lady dressed in a white nightgown and sitting in an even older-looking wicker rocker that I was sure would be auctioned that day. It had been a while since I had seen Maude, and I hardly recognized this person with the wild mass of gray hair. Of course, I probably had no idea what a 101 year-old woman looked like, for whenever I saw her before, she wore old-fashioned clothes and a fancy hat. Mom told me once that she had been a milliner so the hats she wore, often wide-brimmed with lace and turquoise-colored peacock feathers, she had made.

That day, the town centenarian moved to a nursing home in Fair Haven. George said that although she became more and more frail, Maude never quit sermonizing about the sins of liquid spirits and the idle hands of children.

Two other historic characters had been friends for years. Emma Michaels and Sarah Wendell had known each other since they were children. When Emma married, Sarah stood up for her. After the wedding, Emma moved to her husband's farm in the country, but they stayed friends for years. When Emma's husband died, leaving her childless and unable to handle their farm by herself, the two decided to move in together in town and share expenses because Serepta's husband had also died recently.

Their living arrangements seemed to work for a time, but after awhile the two began to feud. So hot were their tempers that Emma had the outhouse from her farm moved into town and set up on Sarah's property. Emma's philosophy was that she might have to share the woman's house, but she didn't feel obliged to share her biffy.

As the sun began to lower in the west window, George drained his coffee cup and reached in his back pocket for his wallet. Myrtle took George's cue to open her purse and search for tip money. After thanks, goodbye, and come again, I watched history walk out the door. I could hardly wait until the next Friday when the lunch crowd brought Clearwater back to life again.

BETWEEN SNAG AND SHORE

A wannigan on the Mississippi at Clearwater

"Necessity is the mother of 'taking chances.'"

-- Mark Twain, *Roughing It* --

Mom told Dad she had enough of crawling out of bed early mornings to flip greasy hamburgers. But she didn't tell him at the time that she had socked away enough of her tip money for a down payment on a house she had been keeping an eye on in lower Clearwater.

Mom knew that Dad, who was usually slow in making decisions and never much of a risk taker, needed a little prodding to get him to agree to buy a house. She got her friends, Joyce and Carl, to help her "work on him" over the summer.

Whenever the three of them had the opportunity, usually late Saturday afternoons when Dad and Carl came in to the café to help Mom and Joyce clean up for the week, they'd start a conversation about the joys of owning a house. Once the proverbial "cat" hopped out of that bag, Dad hollered around a bit saying, "We can't afford it." And "How we ever going to make the payments?" Mom knew this man who'd been orphaned at an early age had a hard time dreaming for the future. But somehow, she got the old man to go along with her decision.

One fall day, Mom brought home her last cash bag. We began to pack up our belongings as we said our sad goodbyes to our tranquil home. I rowed out to the middle of the lake, taking my last look at the dock, the marsh weeds, and the evergreens. For the last time, Becky and I hiked down to the creek. We built a sandcastle, walked across the rickety bridge, and put our feet in the cold water. Even though Carol and I would see each other every day at school and we could call each other whenever we wanted (our telephone numbers were easy to remember: mine was 2475 and hers was 2474), I hopped on my bike and rode to her house to say goodbye.

The night before we left, I walked out to the dock, trying to imagine sparks spitting from the campfire while the girls from Camp Suima sang their farewells.

But there would be other goodbyes. Early that spring, before Mom even mentioned that she wanted to quit the restaurant business,

Donald told us that he had been talking with a recruiter and that he wanted to join the Navy as soon as he graduated in May.

No longer would I be able to get a whiff of spicy English Leather when I dusted his dresser. No longer would he entertain Becky and me by gyrating his hips and lip-syncing to "Little Sister" with Elvis. And no longer would Becky and I whine to Mom or Dad because Don hogged the bathroom when he stood in front of the mirror combing his hair up into a rolled V. Soon our brother would get a new hair cut and begin singing a new song, "Anchors Away."

Donald F. Frank
1963

ANCHORED IN THE STREAM

CLEARWATER UNITED METHODIST CHURCH

"Religion consists in a set of things which the average man thinks he believes, and wishes he was certain."

-- Mark Twain, *Notebook* --

Our home on Spring Street before streets were paved and a small garage had been added

Mom's laborious life as owner, cook, and waitress at her restaurant may have come to a close, but she still needed socialization. Country living, though charming and peaceful, provided her with little opportunity for coffee, gab, and the opportunity to relive history. In the fall of 1963, after she and Dad signed mortgage papers, we traded our friendly green stucco at the lake for a small white bungalow in town, two blocks from the Mississippi River.

Once we unpacked our dishes, set up the beds, laid the large brown and gold braided rugs over the hardwood floors, and arranged the green love seats and chairs in the living room, Mom and Dad began their slow renovation of this sixty-year-old house. Mom stripped the tall mopboards, but once she got down to the wood, she realized that the mopboard needed to be replaced. After she and Dad installed new, Mom painted ceilings and walls golden-yellow and antiqued the kitchen cupboards green, true to 1960's fashion.

Except for our location, our lifestyle changed very little. We still had our same friends, but now they came into town to play 500 with Mom and Dad. Joyce, Carl, SueLynn and Nancy hopped into their '58 black and white, four-door Ford, and drove from their farm out on Highway 7 to our house to partake of Saturday afternoon coffee and cake before heading to either Clear Lake or Kniss' Grocery to stock up on supplies. While Mom and Dad continued the restaurant habit of buying bulk supplies like canned vegetables and fruit in St. Cloud at the Prairie Market Wholesalers, they purchased apples, oranges, lettuce, and Diet RC Cola at Kniss' Grocery.

And I continued attending Clearwater Elementary School. That fall I began eighth grade. I learned beginning algebra under the watchful eyes of George Washington and Abraham Lincoln, who stared down from their blackened-silver frames, and the tutelage of Mrs. Fobbe who felt that it was her duty to prepare us for the next years when we'd be going to junior high in St. Cloud as ninth graders.

But because our family lived closer, we also became more active in the Clearwater United Methodist Church. Like Huck Finn who mulled over the duality of heavenly visions offered by the Widow Douglas and her sister Miss Watson, we sometimes paddled in a stream of mixed currents.

Postcards from the Old Man

METHODIST INCENSE

A congregation of aromas lingers
like incense in the shadowy corners of my mind:

Fugitive bat dung and pungent mold
greet Sunday morning parishioners
when black-suited ushers
swing open the white double doors at 8:45.

Dusty oil when the furnace kicks in
and choking a few of the black-robed choir
singing "Holy, Holy, Holy"
while they marched up the aisle behind Rev. Mary.

Caustic rubbing alcohol fumes
Caroline massaged on a paraplegic's legs
fumigates our family pew,
drugging me to sleep.

Heady brewed coffee
 (one cup of Folgers,
a dash of salt, two eggs—
including shells--
tap water filled
to the white scratch,
boiled in the black-speckled
enamel pot)
wafts to the altar,
reminding black-flocked pastor
his hour is over;
time for the noon potluck to
begin.

Powder clouds
of lavender talcum
puff from Arlene's
swinging arms
leading Sunday School
to "Bring Them In" while she clucks
"Sing the chorus one more time."

Clearwater Methodist Church
1963

Anchored in the Stream

Evening in Paris escapes from Millie's pew,
(front row, right side),
as she belches out the beat
to hymn number 17, "How Great Thou Art,"
(and every other tune that drags).

Spicy English Leather
as Usher Sam bops Dad's arm
during communion if he kneels
meditating too long at the oak banister.

Sticky sweet Welch's grape juice and dry bread cubes
on the breaths of Sunday well-wishers
departing hastily after service so they can get home
in time to take the roast beef out of the oven.

Cigarette haze defects
from front steps to heavens
after the congregation signs yearly pledges
promising not to drink, swear, or smoke.

Musty Crayola wax and bits of wrapper
when the ice cream pail lid is removed,
piles of chocolaty Hydrox cookies,
red rows of sweating glasses of sour Kool-aid
line the basement kitchen counter
on hot summer mornings during Bible School.

Summer's misty heat mingles with flower urns
of baby's breath, roses, and carnations
covering the altar, sanctuary steps, and side aisles
at the funeral of Donald Burns, killed in Vietnam.

"But thanks be to God who . . . manifests through us
the sweet aroma of the knowledge of Him in every place."
                    2 Corinthians 2:14

Postcards from the Old Man

Hotel Scott burned down around 1924

An 1860's picture of early Clearwater Methodism shows parishioners posing on the church's steps beneath a sign that reads "Jesus Saves." This posted claim bore truth for many. When farmers on the county's prairies encountered native uprisings, town citizens followed Benjamin Franklin's advice of "God helps them who help themselves" and built a stockade around the Congregational Church at the top of the hill. Fortified, this building became a shelter for individuals in the area. In addition, a militia from Ft. Snelling was sent to help guard the town. Unfortunately, other "acts of God," some unnatural acts of man, and a lot of Pecksniffian behavior rarely went unnoticed by the Clearwater's righteous.

Fire has always either fanned support or turned adversary; Clearwater was not immune to its carnage. For years, not much could be done when a fire broke out because of lack of equipment to blast water to control the flames. But later, after many disasters, the town invested in a chemical tank with hoses that stretched for blocks. The new equipment took about eight people to operate in order to mix the water and the chemical and blast flames. Before the town installed its official alarm, someone ran into the vestibule of the Methodist

Church, and pulled the rope that rang the bell, warning citizens of imminent danger.

Over the years, many important buildings became historic ashes. In 1924, many town citizens gathered to help put out the fire that engulfed Hotel Scott. Unfortunately, chemicals, water, and personal fortitude left only wet char. Another fire destroyed part of the lumber yard and the elevator that sat adjacent to the railroad tracks. Even old timers talked about how lightning, nature's torch, nearly razed the town around the turn of the twentieth century, burning down many village businesses and the post office. Farmers, far out on the prairie, saw the red glare and rode into town to help put it out.

But sometimes conflagration happened for other reasons. When a disastrous drought hit the area, resulting in a poor wheat crop, the farmers weren't the only ones to suffer financially. The flour mill owners came close to bankruptcy. When a blaze began at the mill, down by where the Clearwater River flows into the Mississippi, those who tried to douse it began to suspect arson when they saw a mysterious red gas can lying tipped over in the weeds. Although no one seriously investigated the inferno, many in town believed the owners started it to claim the insurance money.

Postcards from the Old Man

Clearwater faced other catastrophes. Grasshoppers swooped upon the area in the late summer of 1856, gobbling up corn, wheat, rye, oats, vegetables in people's gardens, and even the sheets, towels, and underwear left to dry on the clothesline after the early morning wash. Although the locusts nibbled at nearly everything and left destruction in its place, the worst was yet to come by the next spring when the eggs hatched in the soil and the only crop big enough to be harvested that summer of 1857 was despair. Many farmers and town citizens left the area, promising never to return. The little green and brown eating machines again hit the region in 1873 and continued for the next five summers, consuming almost everything green and edible. Many local farmers had little success burning out the infestations. Ruined financially, they left Minnesota, declaring they'd never return. Those residents who remained reported that one day in early summer they noticed little dark cyclones spurting up from the fields. Spurts joined together into grasshopper clouds that swirled out of the region the same way they came.

Clockwise from the back left: the Pat Quinn home (now Kitty Kothman Johanson), Pat Quinn's Saloon, Whitney Building, the back of the Masonic Temple, and a hardware store

Anchored in the Stream

Mother Nature flaunted fickleness in other directions as well. At times, the community received little snow or rain, causing the farmers to yield meager wheat and corn crops. Because of the rich farmland, homesteaders diversified, raising pigs, sheep, and cattle that helped them through the difficult times.

But often, since the Clearwater and Mississippi rivers surround the town, flooding occurred when precipitation totals were more than required. One time in particular, rains came in such torrents that water and mud filled cellars and the first floors of homes. In addition, the rain came so hard and fast that the Clearwater dam washed away. This deluge sent Pat Quinn's saloon bobbing down the Mississippi River, causing the pious to send thankful prayers to the Almighty for His highhanded workmanship in the war against evil rum.

Although Methodist services had been held in various locations around town since 1858 when Reverend Levi Gleason conducted the first, no building had been built to house the Lord. Many church members felt this had to be rectified. They hired Civil War veteran Sam Marvin to construct a church. During the war, Marvin had had his thumb shot off, but this didn't stop him from working at his trade and by 1881 church members prided themselves in having a white

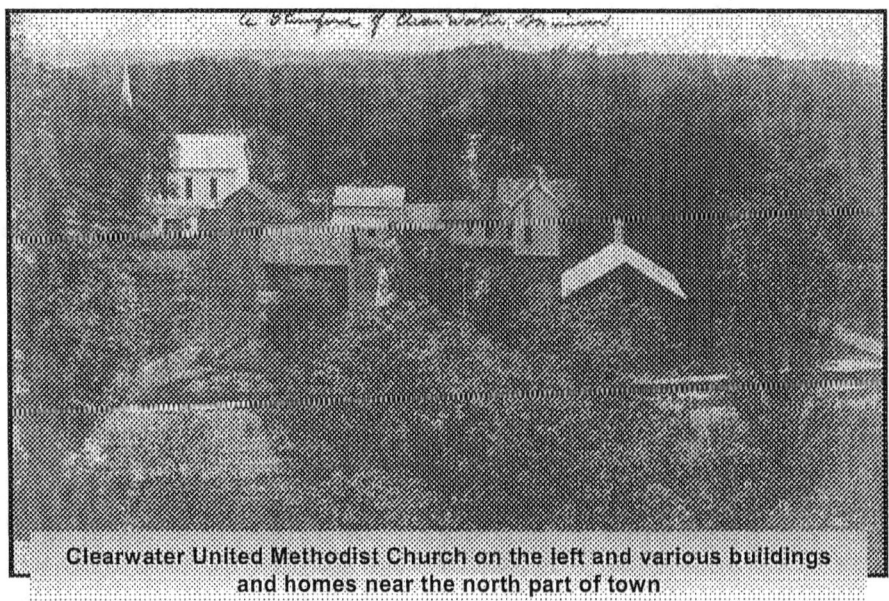

Clearwater United Methodist Church on the left and various buildings and homes near the north part of town

edifice with its steeple pointing to heaven, the way of truth and life.

Many a male pew polisher harmonized "Amens" for their reverend's anointed two-hour sermon over the harmful effects of tobacco and whiskey then proceeded to the front steps to light up cigars and pipes and gulp from the bottle hidden inside the large knot of the old elm shading the church.

A few of the early settlers desired to bring a sense of belonging to those who had been part of the Masons back east. Two energetic individuals, William Tuttle Rigby, and Joseph R. Locke, drove to St. Paul by oxcart, one hundred forty miles round trip, to obtain a request for charter. After they returned to Clearwater, they organized the Clearwater Masonic Temple in 1858. For a number of years, the organization held meetings at various buildings around town until they raised enough money to build a structure of their own. The first building followed the fate of many others in town when it burned down. But the second one, a yellow stone structure, imposed its furtive brow over the southern part of Main Street. By invitation only, many church members became part of this mysteriously secret and sacred order of the Masons. As one of the first orders of business, the early members bought land, about a mile or so north of town, from J.M. Fuller for $100 for a burial grounds and named it Acacia Cemetery. With this purchase, members had comfort in knowing they'd be able to slumber in eternity under the shadows of cedars and oak.

While only men took part in the Masons, both men and women harnessed themselves to the Eastern Star. Even though some citizens who weren't part of the group wondered what secret proceedings went on behind the closed-door meetings, most realized that many members lived up to the organization's sacred mission that encouraged charity, truth, and loving kindness for the good of all humankind.

Few of the early citizens in this river town ever blamed God for plague, fire, flood, or drought. A number of them took seriously the Bible scripture that commands, "Do not let your left hand know what your right hand is doing." And others lived up to Twain's assessment:

"It is agreed, in this country, that if a man can arrange his religion so that it perfectly satisfies his conscience, it is not incumbent on him to care whether the arrangement is satisfactory to anyone else or not."

Postcards from the Old Man

"Spirit . . . has fifty times the strength and staying power of brawn and muscle."
-- Mark Twain, "Saint Joan of Arc," essay 1904 –

Religion is an important part of one's upbringing; I, too, benefited from the indoctrination into the universal Christian family. Each Sunday morning, I sat on one of the red chairs circling a small table in the church basement eagerly waiting for instructions from the teacher to color pictures of baby Jesus, memorize a new verse like "God is Love" from the Bible, or listen to a story. After hearing that Jesus invited the little children to come to Him, I remember looking up at His portrait and thinking I really liked this kindly-looking man. Before Sunday school was ever officially over for the day, we children of all ages and grades climbed the basement steps and gathered in the church pews to sing songs like "Jesus Loves Me," "What a Friend We Have in Jesus," or "Bring Them In" before joining our parents in the family pew to attend church. Long before *It Takes A Village*, I learned the importance of the nourishing church community for a child's soul.

In addition to getting to know Jesus during Sunday school, I learned a number of lessons while attending church. I became educated in when to stand for the "bigger people's" songs like "Amazing Grace," "The Old Rugged Cross," and the "Doxology," which always came after the offering. I also learned how to bow my head and pray the Lord's Prayer and say the Apostles' Creed in synchronization with others. Most importantly, I learned how to be quiet for one hour or more because while the activities that made me stand up and sit down held my interest for awhile, many times the minister's hour-long sermons put me to sleep, literally, with my head on Dad's lap.

Sometime after school let out in the spring and in between swimming lessons during the early part of the summer at the Mill Pond, I attended Bible School where I received more instruction in the Christian faith. Sometimes I received a ride from one of the elderly neighbors, Mrs. Collins, who had volunteered to teach classes for the summer. I waited for her at the end of the driveway. Dust spewed as she pulled up beside me. When I hopped into the back of her 1947 Ford, I smelled dusty rubber as the white-haired lady, with her hands firmly positioned at ten and two, pulled away from our mailbox.

Each summer morning as I entered the cool basement along with other children, I anticipated the special projects the teachers had prepared to keep their classes busy. One year Kay, Barb, and I put together a house that resembled the one where a seriously ill man was lowered through the roof by family and friends because they wanted Jesus to heal him. We followed patterns by cutting out sections of cardboard for the walls and roof. After we colored the sections, we glued the pieces and framed together the structure. We used clothespins for the disciples, drawing faces with crayon and cutting snippets of brown yarn to paste on the top for hair. With Popsicle sticks, we made a cot for the sick man to lie on. This endeavor brought this part of scripture to life.

Although we had plenty of activities to keep us involved, we welcomed the fifteen-minute breaks. About a half hour before we were excused to form a line for our snacks, the scent of tart red Kool-Aid and Hydrox cookies wafted to our classroom. After standing in line waiting for a turn to grab one of the sweaty glasses and chocolate snacks, we went outside to let loose some of our pent-up energy. Often we played hopscotch between the chalk lines the older kids had laid out on the sidewalk. We girls took turns throwing rocks down on squares and attempting to hop to the next square without stepping on a crack or tipping over.

Religious education included becoming part of the church, and Don, who was the oldest of us three children, led the way. Although both he and I had been dedicated at the Baptist Church in St. Cloud when we were younger, when it was time for him to become confirmed under the tutelage of Reverend Gerry Domonosky, he had to be baptized before this could happen. After sister Becky was born 1958, we were sprinkled together.

A few years later, I also learned what it meant to be a Methodist under the watchful care of Reverend Mary McNichol. In addition to learning Bible verses, creeds, and Methodist history, Miss Mac took our group, David, Kay, Barb, Mary Lou, and me, on a field trip to

Minneapolis and St. Paul. We visited the large Hennepin Avenue United Methodist Church. Our little white place of worship paled in comparison to this huge building. We strolled through the sanctuary, taking a few moments to sit on the padded benches to view the different sized organ pipes covering the wall and the huge cross above the altar. Later, we clambered up to the balcony to look down on the sanctuary; this was a novelty for us because we had only a one-story church. Huge portraits of Hennepin Church founders, John Wesley, and Christ filled this upper room area. Once we finished our tour, the minister took us to the main offices where she introduced us to secretaries and other ministers before taking us to the cafeteria for lunch. This visit to an out-of-town church showed me how our small community congregation fit in the larger religious picture.

As a teenager when we lived in town, I belonged to the Methodist Youth Fellowship (MYF), and while many times my mother made me attend meetings, often I felt like I didn't fit in with the crowd. Because I was introverted, many wholesome activities like skating at the Mill Pond and having a weenie-roast over a blazing bonfire with other Clearwater MYF teens became an internal struggle with my self-esteem. When the youth group had the responsibility of designing a nativity set, I hobbled along but felt I was of no use because I couldn't paint, draw, or even cut cardboard in a straight line. At this point in my life, I hadn't figured out God loved all of me, in and out.

One individual showed me that even though I had no hope in the field of artwork, I had other talents. This individual, Greta became a silent mentor to me before many of us knew what the word meant. Always dressed to the nines and her hair done up in a high beehive, she drove around in the same fashion—in a black "Vette." For awhile, Greta was the MYF leader, the choir leader, my Sunday school teacher, and just an all-around inspiring person to be in charge of youth. While she was on duty, I didn't feel like I was one of the silent minorities. Although Mother had always said I had a nice voice, like any other typical teen, I had to hear it from someone else before I believed it. Greta encouraged me to open my mouth and sing a few chords, as well as dress up in a black robe and sing with the choir on Sunday. Attending church took on a whole new meaning for me after I joined the choir.

Anchored in the Stream

Our church didn't seem to have many rules and regulations. I didn't have to prove my faith by memorizing long scriptures, various prayers, or difficult creeds. Our church's basic philosophy seemed to be a universal one: Treat others as you want to be treated. While I know the congregation sometimes had problems--some didn't always get along with each other and others didn't like this minister or that--I was mostly immune to the internal skirmishes as I was growing up. I belonged to a family of believers who were concerned that children learn the way of truth and life. And although I was a typical rebellious teenager, this Christian education provided me with a steadfast faith that has kept me stay on the straight and narrow.

Postcards from the Old Man

A MEASURE OF FAITH

My faith's a sonnet versed in honest doubt.
Bemused by bardic men of ministries
who preach they own the heavens with their clout,
I'm unmoved by
pulpit policies--
attendance, the tithe, last rites
for hidden wrongs.

King James confuses me with
Thees and Thous.
My tongue refrains from
ancient Weslyan songs,
in-unison recited
metered vows,
the babbling and chanting of
such lofty creeds.

But as I choose which Frost-
like path to take,
like wings, His word unfolds
and leads.
Through Psalms and Songs—
a salve for inner ache,
I respond
in syllables to the Lamb
with echoes that praise the Great Iamb[1].

Clearwater United Methodist Church
Artist Billy Auwater

---

[1] A measure in poetry with one stressed syllable followed by an unstressed syllable. This is a play on the Christ's words in John 8:58 where He calls himself the Great I Am.

LEARNING THE RIVER

Mississippi River at Clearwater, Minnesota

"You can't depend on your eyes when
your imagination is out of focus."

-- Mark Twain, *Notebook* --

The Mill Pond on Clearwater River

Now that we were town citizens, I could head to the Mill Pond more often and my journey became easier. In the past when we lived in the country, I had walked or biked (often bucking my little sister Becky on the back of my book rack) over the gravel road, through the grassy car path that cut through Sportsmen's Park, down the steep trail (bypassing the soft sand—a small reminder of the grist mill that once stood near the river), to the girls' swim house to change into my suit for an afternoon of lessons or fun. After we moved into Clearwater, I often escaped the summer's heat, humidity, and housework by walking past the picturesque north end of Main Street on my way to the pond to join up with others in an afternoon of swimming.

This area, a nature observatory, reminded me of snapshots I'd seen of New England's countryside. Overhanging trees of all kinds provided an archway on this street that ran out of town. The algae smell from the green pond on the left side of the street often became so pungent I crossed to the other side in an attempt to escape. But on this side of the road, I had a good glimpse of what locals called Lower

Learning the River

Park. Never as cozy and friendly as the Upper Park or the Mill Pond, this area had charm despite the fact the trees made a stronger barrier against the sun's rays, making the park dark and damp. Depending on the depth of the Clearwater River, the water flowing over the dam could be slow and meandering or gushing and rushing toward the Mississippi. Scenic, yes, but the excitement was on the other side of the dam, across the highway.

The dam at the Lower Park

For decades, Clearwater's youth worshiped summer afternoons at the Mill Pond. Ruth Phillips Sheldon referred to the swimming hole as, "our beloved Mill Pond" in her unpublished book *Memories of Clearwater 1890-1911*. A few generations later, we held the same esteem for this spot and learned to swim from teachers hired by the Red Cross and to play under the watchful eyes of teenage girls, like Kitty and Judy, who not only earned money as lifeguards but had the added benefit of getting beautifully bronzed.

From the time we trained to float for a few seconds as tots until we jumped from the diving board in order to pass swimmers as teenagers, most of us respected the river of different moods. When its tame waters moseyed slowly toward the dam, a few of us girls took breaks from playing on the raft or swimming laps to wander over to the bridge. After looking at Harold Kloevner's carp traps, we'd walk down the steps and through the walkway under the highway where the water made its way calmly to the Mississippi. Frequently, we sat with our feet dangling over the wall, letting the blue-green water run over our feet.

But other times, when the Clearwater peaked, the water rushed to the Old Man. As I swam, I felt its tug and pull. As it angrily gushed down over the walls, I knew better than to stroll under the highway because slippery cement and hurrying water could push me over the dam's edge. Unfortunately, there were a few who didn't have a healthy reverence for this part of the river and sometimes paid the consequences.

No Lake Mead nor Hoover Dam, yet the Clearwater Mill Pond and dam provided plenty of recreation for the town's youth as this small tributary made its way to the Mighty Mississippi.

SHE TEMPERS DULCET CREAMS

SHE TEMPERS DULCET CREAMS
(from Milton's *Paradise Lost*)

Our vestibule's framed greeting,
"*Velkommen in Haus Frank,*"
invites all guests
to gather around Mother's table
to partake of her hospitality.
She creates tempting morsels:
pours eight cups of cold tap water into the percolator,
adds four scoops of Folgers,
piles a platter with cinnamony snickerdoodles
and heavenly devil's food
While her friends wait for the brew's drip, drip, drip,
they indulge in other tasty tidbits:
    the cost of eggs at Kniss Grocery
    Howard's night in jail
    the mayor's slippers under another woman's bed.
As the klatch sips her brew, they snack on:
    Hermosa's hysterectomy
    Mel's stewed state at the street dance
    Sally's six-month marriage and premature baby.
When it's time for friends to leave,
they pick up their napkins,
wiping the crumbs from their lips.
After their "thanks" and her "come again,"
Mother smiles in pride because her guests left well fed.

As a mother and teacher, I know that most young people will do anything to fit in and be accepted by their peers. I behaved no differently. I often bowed to peer pressure and ignored the consequences. Once I agreed to take my first drag on a cigarette by the school house (shortly after I learned to light a match). I also took my first swig of whiskey from a schoolmate's bottle while the two of us sat under the viaduct talking. Another time I crawled into a car so overloaded with other kids that some sat on each other's laps while others squeezed under legs to sit on the floor mats. After we all piled in and closed the doors, the driver peeled out of Dick's Lunch parking lot (<u>not</u> while my mother operated this establishment). He tested his intelligence by speeding over the river's icy bridge. But this test lasted only a few second before he spun out on the highway, sending the car and all of us into a soft snow bank. None of us were injured, but I am not sure any of us learned anything from this escapade except that we were "lucky" because we got away with something without paying the consequences. Even though my parents instilled a moral core within me, I took these chances because like so many young people, I wanted to be liked. Most of the time I had to decipher not only between right and wrong but what was <u>more</u> right or <u>more</u> wrong. And sometimes, even if I chose the right path, I still got in trouble.

One Saturday morning, as gray clouds built up in the west, I asked Mom if Pastor Mary planned on calling off the MYF (Methodist Youth Fellowship) picnic that evening if it stormed.

Mom slid the spatula under a pancake and onto my plate before saying, "I think the church bulletin said that if it rained, the picnic would be in the church basement."

"Oh, geez. Do I have to go?" With my fork, I stabbed holes in my pancake. I hated going to MYF.

"Of course you have to go. Now eat up. We have lots of chores to do. As soon as your finished here, strip the sheets, and get a load of wash started. The sheets have to dry before it rains. There's a good hot breeze outside so it shouldn't take them long."

Learning the River

"Then can Sharon go with me tonight?"

Still standing over the stove with her back to me, she paused before saying, "I don't think so."

"Why?" I whined. "She's my best friend."

After she set the platter of pancakes on the table, Mom looked at Dad peeking over the newspaper. She turned and looked straight at me.

"Sis, sometimes we can become known by the company we keep. I think, that is your father and I think, you have seen enough of Sharon for awhile." She cleared her throat, "We heard a little about her party last weekend…you know…about the excitement that went on in the hayloft."

I had been to Sharon's party. I had been in the hayloft. When Johnny picked up an armload of hay to throw on Sharon, a couple of mice scurried out from underneath another of pile. Some of us girls screamed and raced to see who could get down the ladder quickest. That was the only excitement I knew about.

"Haylofts are no place for unchaperoned teen parties. Besides won't Diane and Judy be there?"

"Geez. They don't talk to me when they are together. No one talks to me when I am there. I don't want to go at all if Sharon can't go with me. I hate MYF." At this point I started crying, " I want to quit."

"Oh, come on now. You have to go to MYF until you are confirmed. Harold, what do you think? They'd just be going to a church outing."

I could tell I was wearing down my mother. After a few pleases, Dad shrugged and Mom said okay. I called Sharon and told her that we'd pick her up at 6:00 and bring her home at 11:00.

Postcards from the Old Man

I was ready at 5:00. I went into the kitchen.

"Sis, go wash that stuff off your mouth right now! You're going to a church outing not a barn dance. While you're at it, put on some jeans instead of those shorts."

Why hadn't my mother figured out I had grown up? I was thirteen, old enough to wear a little makeup and old enough to pick out my own clothes. I stomped back to my room.

Sharon lived about three miles from town. As Dad pulled into her driveway, Mom mumbled about the grass. I looked out the window and saw a lawn mower sitting in tall grass near the mailbox and a little gray tricycle with no handlebars lying sideways under the clothesline. An orange-black cat came out from under the porch carrying something ugly and furry in its mouth.

Dad honked. Because Sharon didn't come out right away, I climbed out of the car to get her. After knocking on the ripped and rusty-red screen door, I peeked in the porch. Flies circled a bag heaped with stinky garbage. Squashed beer cans lay scattered on the floor.

Sharon looked great as she came out the door dressed in her new blue short-shorts I had helped her pick out at Three Sisters in St. Cloud. Her teased, short blonde hair looked real bouffant-like. The heavenly-blue eye shadow I also helped her pick out brought out the violet in her eyes.

After we climbed into the car, my mother asked, "I hope your mother doesn't think 11:00 is too late for you to be out?"

"Mom and Dad aren't home. I called Grandma and told her I was going with you."

With his arm resting on the side of the rolled down window, Dad looked backward as he started to back up the car to return down the driveway. Even though I couldn't recognize his intent, his usually smiling green eyes squinted a dark warning at me.

Learning the River

"It sure is hot and muggy tonight. I wonder if we're in for a storm? Mom asked.

Dad "humphed" and pushed back his wavy, black hair before putting the car in drive and heading back down the dusty road toward town.

I looked at the dark clouds. Mom and Dad said nothing. Sharon seemed nervous because she kept bunching up her shorts with her left hand. I wanted to say something, but thought if I opened my mouth I'd break the fragile quiet.

When Dad pulled into the parking area for Upper Park, Mom opened her car door and got out of the car. She waved at Mrs. Anderson, the MYF leader, and then turned to me.

"We'll be back before 11:00. If it looks like a storm is coming our way, we will be back earlier. Look for us and wait for us here, unless Mrs. Anderson tells you to do otherwise."

I grabbed the tattered blanket from Mom's arm and walked toward the picnic tables. I saw Diane and Judy sitting under a tall evergreen. They waved. Diane cupped her hand and whispered in Judy's ear. They looked at Sharon and I and started giggling. Happy that I had someone to talk to for once, I pretended to ignore them.

While Mrs. Anderson spread a red and white tablecloth over the picnic table, her daughter Charlene unwrapped blue and white plastic bags of hot dog buns.

"Hello girls— glad you could make it. We hope to eat as soon as the fire gets going. Some of the kids are off playing volleyball. If you want, you can join them."

For a while, Sharon and I stood and watched the others swat the ball around. We walked over and leaned against a big old oak tree. I promised Sharon that we'd have fun sitting around the campfire after supper, toasting marshmallows, and singing along with Mrs.

Anderson's son Jerry as he played the guitar. I reassured her that we wouldn't sing just hymns. Jerry knew some of the neatest songs that were on KDWB.

"Do we have to stay here the whole time? Let's go for a walk as soon as we are through eating."

"I don't know. I promised my folks . . ."

"Can't we sneak out when it gets dark? No one will notice. We'll get back before your parents come to get us. Besides I promised Johnny I'd meet him by the store. I think Kurt is coming along too."

At the sheer mention of Kurt's name, I felt a catch in my breath. I had had a crush on him since second grade. He had blonde hair, a crew cut, and an adorable split between his two top teeth. I knew that Sharon had hooked me in her plan. Even though I worried that we'd get caught, I needed no more coaxing.

When we finished roasting our hotdogs and eating chips and beans, Mrs. Anderson said that because it was getting dark and looked like rain, she and Charlotte would clean up. She told us to head to the campfire.

Jerry sat on the rock wall that circled the fire and started to strum "Michael Row Your Boat Ashore." Sharon and I joined in on "Hallelujah" as we took the corners of the blanket and spread it on the ground. The muggy night air became oppressive as it mixed with the heat from the flames. After we sang two stanzas of "Kum-Ba-Yah," Sharon elbowed me. We quietly crawled away as a bolt of lightning shot north to south and orange sparks from the fire cracked and shot up like firecrackers. Jerry strummed a few chords before he sang my favorite Beatles' song, "Yesterday."

As I ran behind her toward the park gate, I looked both ways before crossing the highway. Except for clicking crickets, the night had no other sounds. A slight breeze blew my hair from my face as we ran down the hill toward Main Street.

Learning the River

We entered the alley between the lumberyard and Kniss' Grocery Store. In the dark, I saw a tiny lightning bug. Out from a bush jumped a "Boo!" Gasping to catch our breaths from the long run, Sharon and I screamed. We both giggled when we recognized Johnny and the lightning bug that turned into his cigarette.

"What took ya so long?" Johnny asked as he took a drag and let out smoke rings.

"Oh, we pretended we were religious." Sharon laughed, grabbing Johnny around the neck.

Embarrassed for them, I looked away. "Where's Kurt?"

Sharon giggled again. "You ninny. I just told you that so we could get away from that funeral."

Johnny's hands circled Sharon's waist. He pushed her against the store's outer walls.

"Stop necking in the name of the law," hollered someone from across the street.

Two black shadows walked forward. I recognized Bernie with his black, slicked up hair and Vince because of his goofy grin. High school boys with bad reputations, they both cupped cigarettes as they intruded on our side of the street.

"Hey, what's happening?" Vince asked.

"Do ya' wanna move that inside?" Bernie asked Sharon and Johnny as he made crude hip motions.

Sharon and Johnny laughed.
"I think we should be going back to the park, Sharon." My voiced sounded sappy as it cracked into the quiet, black night.

"Well, if it isn't the little church girl." Bernie mocked.

"I'm going back." I said.

"What's the hurry? It can't be more than 9 o'clock." Sharon remarked.

"Yah, baby. Don't you like my company?" Bernie grabbed me around the waist. I wrestled away from him.

"I'm going back, Sharon. Are you coming with me?"

"Just cool it. We'll get back in time."

I wished I were back at the camp and sitting with Diane and Judy.

Sharon and Johnny kissed again. His hands glided up and down her body, pulling on her clothes. I walked away.

"Hey, we'll walk you back little church girl." Bernie snickered.

"No thanks, I can handle this myself."

I took off down the middle of the street where I felt safest. The tall oaks reached from both sides of the street and met in the middle, creating a dark tunnel. The weeping willow stretching across part of the sidewalk protected pitch-black shadows.

At I past the town hall, I heard the screech of a swing. I thought I heard footsteps and whispering. I ran a half block until I got to the vacant lot that had once been a field, but now waist-high grasses proved the area needed mowing.

The night's thick air made me feel hot and clammy. Lightning streaked across the sky. I swatted mosquitoes that bit my arms and legs. A loud rushing noise made me stop to look behind me. Something moved in the grass. I turned to run, but that something grabbed my ankle and made me fall. A hand covered my mouth; two more hands dragged me further into the wet grass.

"Hey, babe. We just want to have a little fun."

My back hurt from falling. In the dark, I recognized Bernie and Vince.

I muffled a scream and bit at Bernie's cupped hand that covered my mouth.

"Hey, don't get so excited," Vince said.

Bernie bent over me; his breath smelled like a dirty ashtray. Vince snickered while he held down my arms. I began crying.

Bernie whispered, "Okay, okay. We were just horsin' around."

As I ran away, I heard the two boys laughing.

Quietly, I crawled on the blanket. Thunder rumbled and droplets of rain hissed as they hit the bonfire. Mrs. Anderson interrupted Jerry's strumming and humming of "Blowing in the Wind" to say we should head for the shelter of the cars until the parents arrived.

"Where's Sharon?" Mom asked as I opened the back door and threw my blanket on the car seat.

"Her dad came to pick her up earlier," I lied.

I didn't care about Sharon. I just wanted to get home.

"Did you have a good time?"

"It was okay."

"I hope we get home before the storm hits. There's hardly a breeze anymore," Dad said as he turned around in the parking lot.

Once we got home, Mom and Dad raced to shut windows. I went into the bathroom and washed. Once in my room, I slid into my pink baby doll pajamas and flung my bride doll lying in the middle of my bed onto the floor. I pulled down the stiff, white sheets and pink chenille coverlet that smelled like sweet fresh air.

"Hey, hey, sh, sh. Everything's okay. You must've been having a bad dream."

Mom sat on the edge of my bed, untangling my damp hair with her fingers. Thunder boomed and lightning cracked. I tried to open my eyes in the dark, but they felt glued shut. I sat up and put my arms around her neck. She smelled of Ivory soap.

"Dad's been outside looking at the sky. He doesn't think we'll have to head for the cellar," she said, trying to assure me.

I lay back down and closed my eyes, pretending to sleep. Mom bent over and picked up my doll from the floor and set it up on my dresser. She pulled up my sheet, kissed me on the forehead, and quietly walked down the steps. For a long white, I lay awake listening to the rain pound on the roof.

TO LESLIE GORE
(after your performance on the D.C. Mall 2000)

Once upon a white lipstick,

Learning the River

TO LESLIE GORE
(after your performance on the D.C. Mall 2000)

Once upon a white lipstick,
ratted hair, and '62 Impalas time,
girls waited on boys
to ask the important questions:
"May I have this dance?"
"Do you want to go to a movie on Friday?"
"Will you marry me?"
I waited for Greg.

At thirteen, wearing pink champagne lipstick,
I hosted my first party.
Boys in braces asked Dippity-Doed, spit-curled girls
to tootsie to the "Mashed Potato."
Greg sauntered up to spit-curled Kathy,
held out his hand
for her to sashay with him to "It's My Party."
I cried over the punch bowl.

At fifteen, in a yellow
and green paisley tube shift,
I followed spindle-legged Bo onto the crowded floor.
Arms above our heads, we jerked with the Larks.
Then I saw Greg.
My heart thumped as he strolled across the room.
His long, dark eyelashes flashed at me,
but he pulled Sharon onto the floor.
As the 45 spun "She's a Fool,"
Greg backed her into a corner,
nuzzled her teased golden locks.
When the gyration ended,
I joined the wallflower battalion
shoving potato chips and onion dip in my mouth.

Postcards from the Old Man

At seventeen, sporting a bouncy brunette flip,
and donning an orange-knit granny dress,
I danced circles around bashful Buck at the street dance.
A dark shadow stepped from the curb,
sauntered into the middle of the street.
Pausing a moment, Greg offered me a wink.
But with his pointer finger, beckoned sultry Sue
to join him in the Hanky-Panky.
Afterwards, he lead her to his burrow
under the weeping willow,
their steam cooling the muggy night.
I snuggled into a slow-dance with bashful Buck
to "That's the Way Boys Are."

At nineteen,
I went to Cedar Point Ballroom on New Year's Eve.
As I slow-danced with Andy,
resting my head on his shoulders,
I saw Greg in the twirling-silver reflective globe,
standing at attention and twinkling in his Navy whites.
He strolled over, tapped my partner's shoulder to cut in.
Our eyes stared deep into each others.
My sweaty hands met his dry ones.
We swayed to "Maybe I Know."

As the deejay played
"Sunshine, Lollipops, and Rainbows,"
we walked out to his car--together.
I snuggled next to him in the car,
straddling the floor shift.
Once he got me home,
I squished my skirt,
waiting for *the* moment.
As KDWB played "All of My Life,"
Greg pulled me close to his chest,
flipped my hair away from my face,
pressed his lips against mine.

Learning the River

The long awaited moment …
his puckerless kiss,
cold and hard as granite without the sparkle,
exposed the truth.
I closed the door on Greg that night.
For the first time in my teen years
I hummed, "You Don't Own Me."

Postcards from the Old Man

ROSIE and HENRIETTA

Alike as an apple and a chicken feather, two sisters, Rosie and Henrietta, seldom went anywhere alone. Already in their fifties in 1962, the two sisters lived in a gray, two-story house with a screened-in porch. Every Saturday forenoon, they walked their two blocks to Kniss' Grocery. Henrietta pushed the cart while Rosie stocked up on Fairway Foods peas and carrots, a red tin of Folgers, eggs, and butter before checking them off her list. They shared the same pew every Sunday at the United Methodist Church--left side, fifth row, aisle. They attended the same quilting groups, prayer sessions, and anniversary parties, for no one in the community would consider inviting one of the sisters without the other. Our family became close to Rosie and Henrietta and rarely had a birthday party, barbecue, or Friday night trip to Val's Drive-In in St. Cloud for a burger without them. Yet, even though the sisters were almost always together for major social events and had many of the same interests and concerns, these two were complete opposites.

Rosie added the adjunct "and neatness" to the proverb "cleanliness is next to godliness." She made sure both she and Henrietta took baths and worn clean, pressed clothes. But they hardly looked alike. While both ladies stood about 5'6", Henrietta was a bit on the plump side and always wore a housedress with a belt around her middle. Rosie, who stood tall and stick-like and never wore anything over size 5, wore both dresses and slacks sets. Even though Henrietta depended on her blue-rimmed glasses, Rosie only needed her reddish glasses for reading. Another recognizable difference was their "hairs," as Henrietta would say. Rosie wore hers in white soft, peony-petal–like locks and in the same style for the many years I knew her, a reflection of the Jacqueline Kennedy impressionistic period, ear-length, teased lightly and puffed backwards. Henrietta also had downy-soft hair, but she wore her airy-transparent blue locks combed back in tighter waves, with two spit curls on each side of her brow. Frieda, the village stylist, washed, set, and sprayed enough hairspray on their heads every Saturday afternoon for their "do's" to last until the next Saturday afternoon.

Learning the River

The sisters had other contrasting characteristics. Although Rosie was usually the more reserved of the two, sometimes even she could not be held back. Like everyone else, she complained about the motorcycles screeching as they came down the hill, the price she had to pay for a dozen eggs, or how much grease she had to pour out of a pound of hamburger she bought at the grocery store. Rosie had a wide knowledge of Clearwater since she had lived in the town all her life. She knew the stories about the oldtimers. When she and Henrietta came over for coffee and cookies on the back porch, she talked about who she and her sister were related to around town, what old buildings were still standing when they were girls, and the pros and cons of the past and present ministers. She often chastised Henrietta because she had her lipstick on crooked or she hadn't cleaned up the kitchen very well after she finished baking. But there were some topics that made her happy. She glowed when she talked about her niece Molly's children. One time when I commented on how pretty she looked in her high school graduation picture and suggested that she must have had many beaus, she stared into the picture for a moment before her lips stretched in a wide Satin Tangerine grin.

Rosie needed to boss, rebuke, and protect Henrietta. Most Clearwater citizens knew that Henrietta was "a bit slow." Now-a-days, Henrietta would have received special education in school and job training so she could live a different life. But in her youth, at the turn of the century, society's mores held her virtually housebound.

When the women's parents died, Rosie helped Henrietta come out of the closet, out of the house, and into the neighborhood. While the community loved and protected Henrietta, sometimes we who lived closest became frustrated with her, especially when she didn't knock before she entered our home. Instead, she'd swing open the front door, calling out our names one by one, "Winnie? Becky? Cindy?" until someone answered. Then after Mom invited her to have a cup of coffee, she'd start talking. Henrietta had a few subjects she liked to talk about best such as the weather--"It sure is hot outside," or "We could sure use some rain;"--food--"I sure like hamburgers but I hate onions;"--and animals-- "I saw Tuttie's dog run out in the street today," or "Old Mr. Hix had to put his dog Max to sleep," after which she sniffed and choked back a sob. Occasionally, she told a bit of gossip, but most people learned the hard way not to tell her anything. If anyone whispered a juicy tidbit to Henrietta before nine a.m.--Julie and Mark filed for divorce or Verna found Joe up at the Clearwater Liquor cozying up with Donna--everyone in town knew it by noon.

In the vis-a-vis of everyday life, these two sisters led opposite lives. Rosie worked. Every morning, she walked down the street and around the corner to fulfill her duties as assistant postmistress for our small community. She sorted incoming and outgoing mail, doled out postage stamps, and stamped packages. After lunch, Rosie walked up the hill to start her second job as bookkeeper at the plastic plant. On the weekends, she knelt in her garden to plant seeds or pull weeds, bent over a hoe to cultivate the rows, or used the big shears to prune the beautiful pink and white rose bushes that stood next to her house.

Henrietta stayed home. Everyday Rosie left her a list to get done: vacuum, sweep, scour the bathrooms, change the sheets. Because she really liked working in the kitchen, Henrietta also did most the baking and cooking. Rosie usually gave her a culinary-free rein and some spending money for ingredients to make her tempting treats. Henrietta could be relied on to provide goodies for church socials, potlucks, or bake sales. At least once a week on one of her daily visits, she brought us a plate of gooey chocolate brownies or lacy lemon cookies.

But change touches everyone; it touched Rosie amd Henrietta, too. When Rosie turned sixty-five, she retired, which meant more time at home to watch over Henrietta. Everyone in town wondered what Henrietta would have done without her sister all of those years. But no one in town really took much notice of the changes in Rosie after she quit working. Some friends of Rosie's said it seemed as though she had gotten kind of forgetful and had a far-off look in her eyes. Then others noticed that Henrietta began looking a little grimy. It didn't appear that she washed off her makeup; she just added a fresh coat every day, creating quite a brown tinge after a while. Church members began to comment that they found what appeared to be dog hair in Henrietta's baked goods (Henrietta had adopted a dog in town since Rosie's illness didn't allow her to object anymore). It became obvious to most people that Rosie had become unable to supervise Henrietta.

As in all crises, the neighbors bonded together and got the two some help. The county nursing home took Rosie. Henrietta received a housekeeper who made sure she got a bath at least once a week. And, even though many people welcomed Henrietta's daily intrusion in their lives, no one ever touched her brownies again.

Postcards from the Old Man

A WINK FROM THE PAST

With a wink toward the Mississippi River that flows a block away, the arched windows of the yellow-brick Masonic Temple have kept a busy eye on Clearwater for over a hundred years. Once a focal point for the town, the building's sidewalk hosted strangers walking up from the ferry landing, the draymen unloading their goods that arrived from the steamship, and citizens gathering to talk about wheat crops and the price of corn. By the time my family moved into town, the Hall had been sitting nearly empty for quite awhile except for the monthly Masons' meetings. As a youngster, I also strolled down the sidewalk. Staring at my shadowy reflection in the empty windows, I recalled stories from its haunting past.

The Mercantile, located on the west side of building, supplied an inventory of gossip for the town folks. While looking for yard goods, women discussed everything from their husbands' lumbago to the traditional Sunday pot roast, with the most emphasis placed on who attended church on Sunday. Rumor had it that once, on the temple's boardwalk, in broad view of anyone peeking out of the store's window, Henry Nelson supposedly pleaded with Julie Peterson to run away with him. But Julie knew the scandal she'd be creating and leaving for her family to deal with since Henry was a married man.

Learning the River

Even though most people in town knew of this tryst, they respected Julie and the Peterson family too much to bring it out in the open. Henry knew that running away together might be their only hope for a life together.

Apparently, those who watched the scene saw Julie clutch Henry's arm, shake her head left and right, then turn and walk away. Later that day, Henry's sister Emily went out to the pump house and found him hanging from the rafters. Julie never married after that. Some say she mooned for Henry the rest of her life.

When I was just a kid, the east side of the Temple still housed Jonesy's saloon, a brewery of babble. While he poured one foaming beer after another for his thirsty customers, the short, fat bartender in his dirty-white apron pulled tautly under his bulging gut shot the breeze with all of his bar-belly pals. Occasionally, when my dad stopped for a short one, I tagged along, propped myself on a round, red stool, and sipped a Hires Rootbeer from a straw.

The smell of sour brew stung my nose, but Jonesy, with his drooping jowls and three necks that rolled and flapped, intoxicated me with his stories. He jawed about Indian warpaths out in the country during the Sioux Uprising and the tunnel built under the Congregational Church for those who needed a quick escape to the Mississippi River in case the town came under attack. He described Clearwater's early citizens, past and present mayors, and a few ministers so vividly that I felt like I knew them. His way with exaggeration, a slap of his hand against his thigh or a jutting backwards with his plump thumb, made tales come alive no matter if they were a bit tall.

Once or twice, I heard this same impresario of the taproom speculate about the unsolved murder of Alice Leonard. After he grabbed a rag and wiped away the wet beer ring left by a previous customer, he crawled up his stool in the back of the counter and retold the story about the incident that happened over sixty years before.

Postcards from the Old Man

"I heard tell the girl's old man died when she was just a kid. Then when her ma died, she went out to Lynden Township to live with her grandma and aunt," he added.

Intrigued because I lived in Lynden Township too, I leaned in closer to the bar as he chatted. I wanted to ask about the murder site, but I knew better than to speak up, especially in a bar. I hoped one of the regulars would ask the right questions.

"Well, remember old Mick Murphy? He found her lying on the side of the road, out there on what's now County Road 44. He and the family were in the wagon riding home after taking Sunday dinner at his wife's folks' place. Thought they saw a bundle of clothes and blankets on the road....figured someone lost something."

I wanted to hear know more the girl's death. How did she die? Who killed her?

Someone said that he'd heard that the girl had been violated and bludgeoned to death. I wasn't sure what bludgeoned meant, but when a few of the guys at the bar looked at me and then down at their drinks, and Dad shifted on his stool and "humphed," I knew that something horrible had happened to her.

As they continued to mince their words, I pieced together the case myself. Apparently, after climbing down from the wagon and investigating the bundle on the ground, Mick left his family, heading down the road on foot to the nearest farmhouse to get help. On his way, he met Alice's aunt's boyfriend, Luke Markin, who, supposedly, on the woman's beckoning, went out to look for the young girl. Mick said that the man seemed shocked to see him in the dwindling daylight. He also said when he told Markin that he thought the girl was dead, the man told him that "Ach, she must be in a trance."

The two of them walked back to the area where Mick had left his family and the girl's body. Markin bent over and listened to her heart and agreed that she was dead. But when Mick asked what they should do, Markin just grunted and started walking back the way he'd come from. Mick knew that they couldn't leave the body there on the side of the road, but he knew he shouldn't be moving her either. Because it was getting dark, he and the wife wrapped her in their blankets, hefted her up in their wagon, and took off to the girl's grandma's.

They bypassed the dark figure of Markin, never stopping to ask him if he wanted a lift. When Mick delivered the girl's body to her grandmother, he explained how he had found her on the side of the road. He made his condolences and headed on home.

The Stearns County Sheriff and Coroner arrived the next day to probe into the incident. After he and his wife gave their testimonies, Mick took them to the spot where he found the body. Although there had been no rain, the pool of blood that had been there the night before had been washed away. The only evidence that remained by the scene was a crushed hat and a club.

According to Jonesy, the authorities followed a couple leads, but they never solved the case. He said Markin went around the neighborhood the day after the murder telling them that the girl died of heart disease. Although he had an alibi for his whereabouts the afternoon of the murder, many people never trusted him afterwards.

When the story came to an end, Dad swigged down his last inch of beer, helped me clamber down from the bar stool, and tossed a few coins on the counter. Jonesy swiped up the change, hollered thanks, and nodded his adieu. Once outside, as I two-stepped along Dad's long stride, I erupted with a volley of questions.

How far from our house was she murdered?

Not far.

Would he ever show me where they found her?

Someday.

Is that Markin man still alive?

I don't know.

I am sure Dad knew the answers, but to protect my young mind, he remained close-lipped.

In the sixties, after the bar closed and the building stood empty, the shrouding bushes crowding next to the building only added more mystery to the Masonic Temple, especially to those of us kids who had curious minds and mischievous thoughts. We knew that Masons and Eastern Star members met there once a month. We heard they had secret meetings where, during initiation, the lodge members dressed in black robes, carried candles, and chanted a strange and ancient lingo. Because none of us knew what went on at these meetings and didn't know what made the building so mysterious, we decided to find out.

One Halloween evening, after soaping up a few car windows, tipping over the city outhouse, and stealing a pumpkin from Old Man Kloevner's garden patch, we climbed in the Temple's partially open window to investigate. Although we lacked the foresight to bring in more than one flashlight, one of us, conscientiously, remembered a fifth of whiskey. As we tiptoed across the creaking wood floor, we found nothing that seemed too mysterious, just layers of choking dust and clinging cobwebs. Someone hollered "Duck! A car's coming." We stayed close to the floor as the two white lights glared into the building and made its way out of town on Main Street. As soon as danger passed, we continued our escapade. The second floor disappointed us; we found two folded chairs tipped over and a long metal table covered with white butcher's paper.

One of the boys leading the investigation found a candle and lit it, adding a flicker or two for our search as we headed back down the steps and made our way to the cellar. As we climbed down the steps, we ducked low ceilings, brushing against the dank and narrow stairwell. We finally entered a large room with a dirt floor. The flashlight and the small candle became powerless against the overwhelming blackness. When my eyes began to grow accustomed to the dark, I made out a few large rocks—or were they rocks? Legend had it that some of the cellar contained a few graves. I grabbed hold of someone. Another person passed the bottle. Suddenly we heard strange squeaking noises. After a few "Yikes" and "Eeeks," we high-tailed it out of there, holding hands but bumping our heads on the low ceilings.

The Masonic Temple isn't used much anymore except as a playhouse or an occasional directional guide to a stranger searching for a church or someone's house. But I've never heard talk of tearing it down. Locals still walk down the familiar sidewalk, still hear the Mississippi River lap, lap, lap against the shore, see a ghostly reflection of Julie and Henry in the opaque window, and maybe notice a back window ajar because another generation wanted to get to the bottom of the town's folklore.

DRIFTING LOGS

"What, then, is the true Gospel of consistency? Change."
-- Mark Twain, "Consistency"--

Drifting Logs

In Life on the Mississippi, Mark Twain states he knew how to detect changes in the "face of the water." Sometimes it "became a wonderful book—a book that was a dead language to the uneducated passenger, but which told its mind to me without reserve . . . for it had a new story to tell every day." Change is like that. Those who look for adventure feel the current pulling them to new locations.

My brother had felt that tug away from the Mississippi's slow current a few years before--no small rafts, only naval destroyers, cruisers, and carriers to take him around the world: Vietnam to Scotland to the Mediterranean. From riding camels in Egypt to helping haul in the Gemini 8 spacecraft with Neil Armstrong and David Scott still aboard, Don followed his quest for new horizons and new voyages.

I came and went a couple times after high school. In the summers before graduation, I followed the Mississippi to Lake Harriet to work as a nanny for a lawyer and his family. After graduation, because I didn't feel the mortar board of academia pulling me yet, I again paddled back to the cities to live near Franklin Avenue with other Clearwater girls. While the river lapped lazily back home, Old Man Waters flowed harder here.

Each morning as I rode the Metro to downtown Minneapolis to work as a bookkeeper at a title-insurance company, I glimpsed at big city life from the smoke-hazed windows as if I were viewing a motion picture. For the twenty-minute commute, while I often stood gripping the ceiling bar and swinging back and forth, I watched black and white patrol cars in the Hennepin County Medical Center parking lot guard white-capped nurses as they changed shifts. Further downtown, men dressed in gray or black three-piece suits carried briefcases and rolled-up newspapers as they marched to their high-rise offices. In contrast, a few men swigged from brown paper bags, and they swayed and stumbled down the streets. The female brigade, clad in khaki trench coats, carrying umbrellas, and clutching leather purses, tottered to their jobs in spiked heels. Many of them headed to sit on stools behind cages in banks, toil behind desks as bookkeepers or telephone operators, or stand behind jewelry or makeup counters at Dayton's or Donaldson's.

Sometimes coming home at night offered a panorama of sights for this naïve Clearwater girl. Often on Thursday evenings, because the stores remained open until 9:00, I met my roommate Helen for window shopping before heading for a Chinese supper at the Nankin. The chandeliered and red-silked atmosphere offered us a safe haven from the rest of Hennepin Avenue. After we finished our sweet and sour pork and fried rice, we walked down to the corner to catch our bus. Except for the lights from the cruising cars, the bars with their flashing Grain Belt Beer signs, and magazine stores with their glowing XXXs, nights seemed blacker here than at home.

On any given evening, we viewed a variety of scenes. Leaning against light posts, bleached-blonde babes bared glowing white legs below mini-skirts to a gaggle of males, old and young, cruising the street and honking their car horns. Squatting against the Big Boy restaurant, blue, pink, yellow tie-dyed teens with matted hair and dirty feet held up a signs that read "Give Peace a Chance." Defending their territories, big burly male bouncers dressed in black leather pushed open bar doors and tossed rowdy drunks out on the sidewalks.

I eventually tired of big city life and moved back home to start a whole new experience. I joined the Northern States Power Company at the newly built nuclear plant at Monticello that stood at the edge of the Mississippi. At first, I helped Diane, the plant receptionist and secretary to the superintendent, by typing instructional manuals and other correspondence.

By the following summer, Diane left to get married and I acquired her position, which broadened my experiences. This male-dominated environment, a combination of General Electric, Bechtel Construction, and Northern States Power employees, left me as the only unmarried woman afloat in a sea of nearly 4,000 men. I met many people, including notable VIPs from all of the United States, atomic energy commissioners, presidents of large corporations, senators and congressmen, including Walter Mondale, our future vice-president. I had to receive all of them because no matter how important they were they had to sign in at my reception desk. In addition, one summer I watched a daily stream of anti-nuclear protesters carrying nuclear warning banners that read "Say NO! to Nukes."

While a flotilla of engineers and construction crews filled the site, I dated only a few because I was just too busy. Instead, I typed first and second drafts of the startup manuals for the site's operation. My change in careers affected my mother as well. Not only did she hold down a job at the Clearwater Plastic Plant, but she also cooked, cleaned, and ironed for me because I worked so many hours of overtime. Although many nights I dragged myself home and fell asleep while trying to eat the supper she had prepared, I socked away extra cash to purchase a brand new apple-green Plymouth Duster.

This big purchase that I made toward the end of November 1970 brought many changes to my life—independence for one thing. I no longer waited for friends to pick me up to go shopping or dancing at the Bucket in St. Cloud. I now drove myself back and forth to work, shopping, friends' homes, and even I took turns picking up others for parties and dances.

But owning my own wheels also brought me hardship. One cold, slippery morning, I headed to the Stearns County Courthouse in St. Cloud to buy my new license plates. As I approached my usual turn-off to Clearwater Road, I decided not to take the less-traveled road, figuring that the longer route had more traffic and less ice cover. I hadn't gone far before I saw cars parked in a string down 152. I pumped my brakes to a stop and parked behind a red Chevy, wondering why traffic had delayed. I searched the oncoming traffic lane and spotted a huge, white semi jack-knifed with its trailer straddling the ditch and its cab tilting sideways. With my foot still posed on the brake, I glanced in my rearview mirror and observed a white car approaching, fishtailing as it came up behind me at a crazy speed. Within a matter of seconds, the car shoved me into the right side of the car in front and then into the ditch.

Although at the time I felt shock but no pain, I had no idea how this accident would alter my life for a time. I crawled out of my bludgeoned new car, walked to a neighboring house, and asked to use the family's phone to call the police, my father, and a tow truck. Except for some weakness in my arms and legs I felt fine. When I arrived home an hour or so later, my neck, front and back, began to ache. I took a couple aspirin and tried to relax. Sleep didn't help. When I awoke the next morning, I had a hard time holding up my head.

My mother made an appointment for me to see the doctor, assuming he'd give me a few muscle relaxants and pain pills, but he had other plans. After x-rays, he ordered me to check into the St. Cloud Hospital where I stayed for twenty-three days in neck traction and received heat and massage therapy. The hot pack shawls nearly scalded my neck while the traction belt, placed under my chin and hooked to 10 pound weights in back of my head, gave me black and blue marks on my jaw line. While I lay in pain and discomfort, the Plymouth dealer, and I mean the owner of the dealership, visited on occasion to get the plans in line for me to sign over the car to him so he could in turn sign it over to the local technical school to repair for resale. In exchange, I received a brand new red Duster that sat in the hospital parking lot for me to drive home when they discharged me.

And the St. Cloud Hospital eventually discharged me, but driving became much more of a challenge and a job that I took more seriously. As I pulled out of the hospital's parking lot, my right foot pounced back and forth from the gas pedal to the brake pedal, fear and fortitude monitoring my driving. At every stop sign and light change, I searched the rear view mirror for enemy cars approaching too fast from behind.

I finally regained my driving habits and became more adventurous. One time after a night of dancing, friends Nancy, Joanne, Donna, and I sat at our booth sipping our white-crowned mugs and grumbling about the same people being at the same hangouts, being asked by the same beer-laden guys to shake our booty to "My Sweet Lord" or "Jeremiah Was a Bullfrog." We wanted to get away and experience new life.

Drifting Logs

I volunteered to try to get the services of my cousin Tom who was stationed at Ellsworth Air Force Base near the Black Hills in South Dakota to line up each of us with a guy for a weekend. The girls jumped at this opportunity. I wrote Tom a long letter describing each one of us. Donna stood tall and thin, wore her long light brown hair straight. Joanne also stood tall and wore her shoulder-length dark brown hair either flipped up or combed under. Nancy, taller than me, had nearly black hair and a healthy physique. Tom knew what I looked like and I threatened him with telling his mother and his aunt, my mother, if he didn't fix me up "good." He wrote back saying that he had guys in mind and we set a weekend for our blind dates.

After a pat on the shoulder from my boss Chuck and a tad bit of male wisdom, ("Don't do anything I wouldn't do" and "Oh, who knows, you'll probably meet the love of your life"), I took off for the weekend quest with my three friends. We had no idea how far the central part of Minnesota was from Rapid City or how long it would take us to drive there. What seemed like only a few inches on the map turned out to be nearly seven hundred flat, treeless miles, a long way from our meandering and fertile Mississippi. We stopped often for Cokes and potty breaks and finally, after thirteen hours, we arrived at the designated hotel, the Holiday Inn, on the south side of Rapid City.

After we registered for our rooms, I called Tom at the base, nearly ten miles away, to set the plan in motion. He said that he and the guys would meet us in a couple hours. Donna, Joanne, Nancy, and I showered and primped. As if we were working a crap shoot, the four of us knew one of us could possibly be a winner before the weekend ended.

Soon the guys arrived; Tom and I were the only ones to hug. He introduced himself, Duane, Steve, and Frank. I introduced myself, Joanne, Donna, and Nancy. At this point, no one knew who was paired with whom. Mostly, the other three couples listened to Tom and me talk about mothers, cousins, and our grandparents while all the rest eyeballed each other, wondering how their elusive dates would turn out.

After Tom asked if we had any ideas about what we wanted to do, I responded that we had decided we wanted to do some sightseeing. We headed out to the Holiday Inn parking lot. Obviously, all us of couldn't pile in one car so Tom and Frank said they'd drive. Since no one knew exactly how we had been paired, we waited for instructions from cousin Noah who paired up this ark. None came. A few awkward moments of wondering elapsed before Joanne said she'd ride with Tom. Donna and Duane said they'd go in his car too. Seeing what the rest had done, Nancy, Steve, and I hopped in Frank's car and took off.

Drifting Logs

THE RECRUIT
Ellsworth AFB, May 1971

When you marched tall and straight into my life,
wearing button-fly jeans and navy-blue tee-shirt,
I tried not to worry about this blind date.
While cousin Tom introduced girls to soldiers
for this weekend furlough,
I tried not to stare at your bronzed and brawny forearms
as you bivouacked into a protective corner chair.
Your gold-rimmed glasses framed wearied eyes;
fist shot up to hold a yawning jaw.

After our party agreed to maneuver in the Hills,
you volunteered to drive your spit and polished,
vacuumed and Simonized '68 Fury.
Men joined ranks, rode shotgun,
WAACS mobilized in back—
A short détente before our troops regrouped.

Most of us filed out at Custer Park
to stretch and view a militia of buffalo,
pet a platoon of burros pillaging food,
but you foxholed in your car.
A furry brown donkey started its reconnaissance.
Nostrils pressed against the spotless window,
smearing snot in raucous circles.

You jerked open the door,
brutishly shoving the animal away.
After a volley of profanities,
one of the asses went AWOL,
And, my dear, I <u>almost</u> decided you were 4-F.

Postcards from the Old Man

Although I <u>didn't</u> declare Frank 4-F, I had no idea how fate would intervene in one river girl's life. Since most of us hadn't eaten much that day, we decided to head back to town before we continued with any more activities. Tom said the pancake restaurant on Rushmore Road had the best menu for an early supper. We headed in that direction, but once we arrived, we endured a few awkward moments in this match game. Tom directed us girls to slide into the long narrow booth. With a little nudging, Tom guided each guy to pull up a chair across from his date: Duane and Donna, Steve and Nancy, Frank and me, Tom and Joanne. I think most of us took refuge behind our huge plastic menus for a few moments to collect our thoughts.

Outgoing Joanne, in-control Tom, and gregarious Duane kept the conversation going. After the server took our eight orders of cheeseburgers and fries, flirtatious conversation circled the table like a round robin. Tom and Joanne talked golf. Duane, apparently a baseball fan, kept us laughing as he filled in with his "Joe Garagiola is my hero!" (apparently, a famous Missouri brother).

Up to this point, Frank and I hadn't enjoyed much one-on-one conversation, but we began to take turns telling each other about ourselves. I told him I was from Clearwater and he told me he was from Ely, in northern Minnesota. I told him about visiting his town a few years before and being curious about whether the canoe outfitting store still had the poor bear in a cage out on the sidewalk. He laughed and said no, an animal rights group righteously forced the owners to free the creature. Then he told me he had made staff sergeant and had been stationed in a number of locations including Las Vegas and Thailand. I told him that I had recently been in a serious accident with my brand new vehicle and I found out from him that he had purchased his green Sport Fury the year before and he liked to spend time cleaning it (and so I had surmised by the little stint at Custer State Park).

After we gobbled our early supper, someone came up with the idea to go golfing. Recently, a friend from work had tried to teach me how to play, but I never saw the point of clutching the club to my wrists, straightening my elbows to the point of pain, aiming the club at a little white ball that, hopefully, got as close to a little black hole way down at the end of the green--all during the wet heat of the summer. Frank said he didn't golf and asked if I wanted to go for a walk.

While Cupid's arrows hadn't had time to pierce any of us this early in our relationships, one of the couples didn't get on at all. Talk of golfing and long walks gave Nancy and Steve the first opportunity to split, both feigning tiredness. So after paying our restaurant tabs, most of us aimed in different directions: Tom, Joanne, Donna, and Duane to play golf under the stars and course lights, Frank and I to stroll around the eastern part of Rapid to talk about nothing, the sleepyheads to rest in separate bunks and dream of other dates. In just a few short hours, one couple bowed out which left three to go.

Most of us didn't sleep much that night, knowing that our time together would end in a few hours and we women would be climbing back in the Duster to head east. But something started that weekend and three interested guys asked if they could come to Minnesota to spend a weekend with three interested girls. Two weeks later, over Memorial Day weekend, Tom, Duane, and Frank, roles reversed, aimed Frank's car east out of Ellsworth, and headed toward Minnesota. As soon as they pulled into our driveway, they dislodged themselves from the cramped car. Duane began his familiar litany: "Joe Garagiola is my hero." Tom tattled about a highway patroler in a bad mood who had stopped Frank on the interstate and given him a $75 speeding ticket. Despite the sad news about Frank having to pay a fine, Joanne, Donna, and I could tell we were in for a fun weekend.

We had planned ahead somewhat, at least what food and refreshments to have on hand for munching and slurping: fried chicken, baked beans, potato salad, and of course, Cokes and beer. Joanne said that one of our favorite dance clubs would be hosting a live band. The guys deferred to whatever we wanted to do so we made plans to go to St. Cloud. While the reflective globe swirled in the smoky gray room, we swooned and bobbed, drank beer and laughed while the band played its renditions of our favorite songs.

WHITE LACE AND PROMISES

You'd cut in on Karen and Richard's tune;
"We've Only Just Begun" played while we danced.
No Ginger Rogers or Fred Astaire—yet June
peach-shaded moon abetted our romance.
While we swayed in three-step harmony,
night began to fade into each song.
Our solstice tryst, now silvered in memory,
hides in shadows when nights grow cold and long:
I measure singleness in short refrain —
recall your caressing arms from long ago,
then move across the room to break the strain
that caused our lyric-strained scenario.

Again we'll waltz before the rising sun.
Despite the years, we've only just begun.

Drifting Logs

By the time the guys had to leave the next afternoon to head back to Ellsworth, Tom and Joanne, and Duane and Donna had developed friendships and had decided to meet up when the two girls and their families camped in the Hills over the fourth of July.

For Frank and me, the twirling mirrorball hanging from the dance hall ceiling had illuminated more than friendship. My folks noticed the sparks and invited Frank to stop back for a visit on his way home to Ely when he was discharged from the service the end of July, but Tom reminded us that we'd see him earlier than the end of the month. He said he'd be back for Grandma and Grandpa's Johnson's fiftieth wedding anniversary and suggested that Frank ride back with him. Frank thought he might be able to come even though once he returned to Ellsworth, he would be getting discharged and would turn right around and head back to Minnesota. I figured if Frank were willing to drive all the way from Rapid to Clearwater to meet my relatives, turn around and drive back to Rapid, get discharged, pack up his belongings, and head back to Clearwater all within a matter of 72 hours, he must be feeling the same as me.

But the end of July was a long way off from Memorial Day and I worried about how this new relationship would handle a two-month separation. Even though we promised to write, I wasn't sure he would. I had been down this proverbial creek before.

For the next couple months, I tried not to muddy my brain with fear with "he loves me, he loves me not." I took a couple golf lessons from a male co-worker. Even though he drove a flashy, red convertible, neither of us felt a flicker between us. By now, Nancy had decided her guy was Bill and she needn't fish anymore. This left Joanne, Donna, and me to resume our weekend pit stops at either the Bucket or Bricky's. I am not sure if Donna and Joanne enjoyed the game, but I found this upstream paddle futile. But I concentrated hard on staying busy and not obsessing about this nebulous relationship.

I don't know who wrote first, but I soon received a two-page letter from Frank. He said he had always "had a hard time trying to write letters," but he'd give this a try. He said on their way back to the base, they ran into bad weather out of Dawson and "had to slow down to forty mph in a sixty-five mph zone." Once the weather cleared, he hit the metal. He would like to see me again soon, but he had "a $200 car insurance premium due July 9th. That kind of socks it to any extra money. If I had the money, I would drive 10 1/2 hours again."

I responded to his letter. I told him that while I regretted that we couldn't get together, I understood money issues perfectly and reminded him of my folks' offer for him to stop in Clearwater on his way back to Ely after his discharge. I said Joanne, Donna, and their families had plans to camp in the Hills over the Fourth. I also told him they'd meet up with him during that time. Otherwise, I had little planned and would probably take my little sister Becky to Annandale for the town's annual July 4th celebration that included the Ferris Wheel, merry-go-round, cotton candy, and late night fireworks. Before I signed off, I took a brazen step and told him that I looked forward to meeting him again.

For someone who didn't like to write, Frank sure wrote back fast enough to tell me about his holiday off; this time he wrote a three-pager full of information about himself. "Duane and I went to the car races. On Monday I took my pistol and went hunting. Half way there, I thought I blew my water pump. Luckily, it was only the thermostat. Had to turn back and replace it. Finally, I made it to the woods. Got two squirrels."

He went on to say he was waiting for the moving van to haul some of his belongings back to Ely. He didn't have much, just clothes and skis (another bit of information: he skied). He told the story about the first time he went to Terry Peak and how he "went in the ditch three times that day . . . All in a mile stretch of road [and] uphill" because he was too cheap to buy snow tires. He closed with "I'll be driving up on that weekend [for Grandma and Grandpa Johnson's anniversary]. No tickets this time." I felt hopeful that Frank had decided to join Tom for the weekend trip, but bewildered that this trip was important enough for him to drive to Minnesota, back to Ellsworth, and then back to Minnesota, thirty-plus hours of driving within a matter of four days.

Drifting Logs

Unfortunately, even though I kept busy, the three weeks before I would see him again seemed like I had embarked on a slow-moving raft to travel from Lake Itasca to New Orleans. I met with Joanne and Donna who returned home from the trip to say, in fact, they had seen "the guys." Neither of them really thought their relationship serious and had made no plans to see Tom or Duane again. Did that mean three couples down, one to go?

Although I remained busy on the job, Mom kept me busy at home as well, helping with the anniversary plans. I helped proofread the program. Because I had a car, she didn't have to wait for Dad to drive her to pick up party supplies. After work and on the weekends I ran errands, picking up napkins, paper plates, and plastic spoons and forks. Mom asked our church quartet, Kitty, Becky, Laurie, and me, to lead the guests in a sing-a-long. We spent a couple Saturday afternoons practicing the verses to "Let Me Call Sweetheart," "Shine On Harvest Moon," "Silver Threads Among the Gold," and "The Church in the Wildwood" (the Little Brown Church in Iowa where Grandma played organ when she was younger).

Frank and Cindy at Johnson grandparents' 50th wedding anniversary party

A few days before the celebration, company started to arrive. First, Mom, Becky, and I drove to St. Cloud to pick up Grandma Johnson's sister Aunt Merle from the train. This plump, great-aunt with blackened hair, jiggled and giggled as she walked. She tattled about her siblings and her in-laws, as well as the rest of the relatives she left back in Longview, Washington.

Postcards from the Old Man

    Although I enjoyed catching up on the lives of relatives and looked forward to the grandparents' celebration, the reunion I had been waiting for finally happened. Frank and Tom arrived late Friday night about the same time many other relatives found their way to our house. Frank and I shared a few minutes of communication before he tucked into my sister's bed and I went off to my own.

    The next day offered the same challenges. Mom kept Frank and me busy. We picked up the cake, helped set up the brown folding chairs, covered the tables with cloths. The afternoon gala event went well, even if Frank and I had little private time.

    The next morning before the guys drove off, Tom revealed the truth about his matchmaking skills. Apparently, the blind date he had lined me up with back in May had received orders to go overseas the week before we arrived. He informed Tom that he was taking leave to go home to see his family and wouldn't be around for the weekend. Tom knew he had to find someone to balance our party. One afternoon he bumped into Frank. He asked him if he had anything important going on for the weekend and if he'd like to go on a blind date. Less than enthusiastic, Frank agreed to join the group. Up to this time, not even Frank knew he had been a fill in.

    Had fate intervened in our lives? All I knew was even though Frank was leaving with Tom, he'd promised he'd be back in a few days. I had no idea who was piloting this ship, but I couldn't wait to pack my bags and hop aboard. Frank returned in three days; within five months, on December 18, 1971, we married and moved to Ely where he worked for the city and the post office. This small tourist town in northern Minnesota became just the first place we would drop anchor on our voyage together.

Drifting Logs

"Change is the handmaiden Nature requires to do her miracles with."
-- Mark Twain, *Roughing It"* --

I could tell Frank wasn't satisfied being a snow remover or postal worker in Ely for the rest of his life. He needed more adventure. I encouraged him to go back into the service. After living only a year and a month in his hometown, he committed himself to another four years in the military. In 1973, when I was eight and a half month's pregnant, we finally started on our long-awaited honeymoon as we drove to Biloxi, Mississippi, where he'd receive more training. Here our first child, Todd, was born in a military hospital. Six months later, we moved to Klamath Falls, Oregon. Three years later, I gave birth to our second son, Matt. When the military decided to close the base, Frank had a choice to either be transferred to a new department and move to Germany and then take his turn on a remote base in Greenland or Alaska for a year or end his stint. Neither of us entertained the thought of his being gone for a year so we took the early out. After being gone nearly five years from my small community by the river, I returned with my family. While these two children altered our lives, Frank and I seldom waded in stagnant waters too long.

We both felt cast afloat without the structure of the military. Frank tried his hand at cash register repair, but the pay kept us one stop away from food stamps. Then he had the idea of starting "Frank's Electronic Business" out of our tiny two-bedroom apartment. Often when I got up in the night to check on the children, I stumbled over stacks of televisions, stereos, and radios that he had piled on top of each to fix. This endeavor also proved futile. Next Frank took a job with an electronic repair shop with the owner's promise that he could make as much as he wanted. This employment opportunity offered us as much hope as the cash register repair business. Often times, my folks bought a quarter or half of beef and donated part of their purchase to our worthy cause.

When our situation seemed the murkiest, the fog began to lift. I encouraged Frank to go back to school to learn a useful trade. With a bit of trepidation, he registered at St. Cloud State University in the engineering program. Even though the G.I. Bill helped, we struggled to pay all the bills and put food on the table. Wanting to help out financially, I struggled over looking for a job when I felt I needed to be home to care for our two small children. Paying a large chunk out of my wages for a babysitter seemed illogical. By spring semester, an ad in the classifieds caught my attention. A local real estate agency needed caretakers for one of its apartment complexes. After I prodded him a bit, Frank made an appointment for an interview. They offered us the overwhelming job of managing and maintaining nearly one hundred apartments.

Although this employment opportunity took almost all of our time because we were on call twenty-four hours, seven days a week, it provided many benefits. Money, for one. With Frank's tuition assistance and the wages we both received as caretakers, we felt for the first time since we had moved back to Minnesota that we could take care of ourselves financially. While one of us did our chores, sweeping and mopping entryways, wiping down laundry rooms, or vacuuming the hallways, the other watched the children. Even though my folks and sister often helped out by taking the boys to Clearwater for a day or two, this job provided us flexibility. Frank could go to school and study. We both could do our jobs, and be with our children, without paying a lot for daycare.

Nearing graduation, Frank's and our future seemed promising. He mailed résumés to a number of places and received a few offers (Boeing in Washington, McDonald Douglas in California, Midland Ross in Mankato, and Brown Boveri Turbomachinery in St. Cloud). Maybe because we liked our comfort zone, he accepted an engineering position at the Swiss-owned, Brown Boveri. At this time we made plans to follow the American dream of owning our own house. We contacted a contractor who helped us design a country home. When we moved to St. Stephen in January 1982, we closed the chapter on our caretaking experiences.

Unfortunately, we plunged into one of the darkest periods of our married lives. Frank's company, caught up in the early 80's recession, pulled its business out of the country and back to Switzerland, putting a couple thousand individuals out of work. We knew we weren't alone in this unemployment tragedy. At the same time, Great Northern Railroad also laid off another couple thousand individuals. A respecter of no one, Reagonomics caused many men and women close to retirement to lose their jobs. My sister Becky, who had graduated with a degree in social work from SCSU at the same time as Frank, also lost her job in Alexandria during this time.

Inundated with house, car, and other bills that run a home, we both felt pulled into the river's deepest sediment. For nearly three years, we struggled to pay bills, look for jobs, and survive. Finally, on what I referred to as Black Monday, as bill collectors pulled harder on the ropes of our horns, I looked up on the wall at an Italian oil print. Brother Don had picked up this painting when he visited Naples. Sometime later, Mother had had it framed with decayed-red wood from Grandpa Johnson's barn. I had loved this picture and since Don hadn't claimed it, I decided it would go very nicely in my living room. While I appreciated the colors the unknown artist had used--oranges, browns, and maroons--my eyes focused on a lone boat tied to a dock on the shoreline. On this day, though, I looked at the horizon and saw a thin brush stroke of pinkish sunrise where sea met sky.

As I stared at that symbol, I felt the fog lift. I had no clue at that point how our financial mess would straighten itself out. Two days later, Frank received a phone call from the company out of Mankato that he had turned down for a position four years before. After he and the personnel director talked, they set a date for Frank to come look over the company. He primped and prepared for the interview, drove the three hours to get there, gave his very best engineer-speak, and before he left, those in charge offered him a job.

We had little to contemplate; we knew that he had to accept the company's offer and make plans to change the course of our lives by moving again. Frank found a small apartment to live in temporarily and came home on the weekends. We contacted a real estate agency and put our house up for sale. While we waited a few months for our house to sell, we made plans to relocate, enrolled our boys in school, and registered me for classes at Mankato State University so I could follow my dream.

It didn't take long before we saw a bend in the river. One weekend Frank came home and said the company had decided to relocate us to Watertown, South Dakota. After an eight-year layover in Minnesota, we heard another boarding call.

Becky, too, became employed and found an apartment nearer her new job. For the first time in a number of years, Mom and Dad had the house to themselves. Soon, though, they also decided to change directions by downsizing, selling the house, auctioning their belongings, and moving to an apartment in St. Cloud.

The folks called one of the local auctioneers who came and looked over their belongings. Days days before the sale, he and his clerks inventoried Mom and Dad's possessions and divided them into stacks.

Harold on auction day

Drifting Logs

THE SALE

A blue-jeaned, cowboy-booted man
hopped aboard the hay rack, hypnotized the crowd
with his "Whad'ya'say? Whad'ya'say? "

Microphone in one hand,
he grabbed a box of clinking Mason jars in the other,
yodeled, "Whooo'l start the bidding?"
Give me dolla' a dolla; whoooo'l give me a dolla?"
He began bargaining for the jars once filled
with plump red tomatoes, pink applesauce,
and stringy-green beans I had turned up my nose to
but nourished our family when the land lay barren.

One of his helpers hefted the galvanized wash tub,
angled, twirled, and flipped this vessel to prove
"It's in good condition, no rust, no holes.
Let's start the bidding at five."
I pictured it filled with sudsy water for Saturday night baths,
heaping with sheets and pillow cases that had slid from the wringer,
or overflowing with ears of corn for the calf.

The broker's voice slowed
as he examined the "good looking" dining table--
shiny-black walnut finish, two extension leaves, sculptured legs.
But he couldn't describe my five-year-old head
stuck between the inner foot supports,
a brainless moment at thirteen when I whittled
my name in the wood and dotted the "i" with a heart,
notebooks and textbooks spread out for a night of homework,
or Simplicity tissue laid over purple velvet for a bridesmaid's dress.

From the tied bundles of gold drapes and checkered tablecloths
to the dirt-encrusted shovels and green hoses,
buyers enthusiastically waved their numbers for the bargains.
As he slowed his squall to "going once, going twice, gone,"
the hammer settled the price for the woman in red
who wouldn't let her youth be sold.

Harold and Winnie after they moved to St. Cloud

After the auction, the folks traded their humble abode in Clearwater for an apartment in St. Cloud where they continued their lives, never leaving Clearwater too far behind because they still remained friends with so many. Without yard work and clothes to hang, the two led near-carefree lives as they travelled around the countryside, but now both took their turns as back-seat-drivers when Mom finally obtained a permit. From St. Cloud to Bayfield, Wisconsin, to take in the scenery, to Watertown, South Dakota, to visit the grandchildren, or to Benson, Minnesota, to visit Becky, Mom never allowed Dad to sit idle too long.

But like our dear Mill Pond that had changed its course a number of years before making it inaccesible to swimmers, my Dad, too, began to follow a different route.

PLAY WITHIN A PLAY

Like a dramatic actor upon the stage,
Dad reenacts a different age and time.
The story begins in the April of his prime
leading us on a road tour
toward the "home."

Exposition act: an orphaned child
fostered on Dakota prairie fields,
small crop of love reserved
for spring wheat yields
for cousins to this German-Russian boy.

Harold and Winnie shortly before they were married

Foreshadowed to own a farm,
Dad moved away.
Bought pastoral scenes he'd sow—then reap;
mowed the hay that fed the cows, the sheep;
curried his beloved horses King and Mike.

The hook: Dad met a woman across the road.
In flirting dialogues, discovered their fate,
courting and cozying until they set a date
for January first to exchange their themes of love.

Rising action: actors join the cast.
Dad quit the farm to pour the lava flows
in rings of iron molds he'd count in rows,
returning at night in mask of black and white.

Climax of the plot: low cash and teens,
who overacted with theatre of the absurd.
Histrionics' showdown, Dad gained last word
in soliloquies he stated repeatedly.

Postcards from the Old Man

Falling action: kids grew up and left.
Dad and Mom retired. Their interlude
cut short by tragic strokes that changed his mood
to a private madness long prevailed.

In denouement, Dad prattled double sense.
He pensioned a sentimental point of view,
rehearsing the roles he played as if on cue:
farmer, husband, foundry man, and Dad.

END OF TERM

Dad fell at the nursing home;
the ambulance siren whirled as they sped him to the hospital.
Quick-stepping nurses stuck him to tubes connected to IV's,
paddled him to machines that monitored his heart.
Mom thinks I should come home. . .just in case.

Quickly, I calculate A's through F's --enter in grade book.
paper-clip compositions, lay them away in a stack --
no time to make them bleed red.
I contemplate lesson plans, figure one week . . . just in case.

I toss clothes by sevens in the suitcase:
socks, bras, underwear, sweatshirts, jeans. . .black dress.
By 6:00 a.m., I take the gray, two-lane curve out of town.
Three hours of white lines, and no passing zones ahead.
I press the cruise to 65 in a 55;
dial the radio in to Minneapolis's 830, WCCO.

For the thousandth time,
Boon and Erickson sing their catcall:
"Good Morning, good morning.
We've danced the whole night through . . .
good morning, good morning, to you."

Over the years, I've learned to tolerate these two.
I shift back to the 60's when I am 19.

The green kitchen radio wakes me;
the tomcats sing--oh, so early.
I punch the pillow, cover my head with blankets,
wait for Dad's wakeup yell. It comes.
Groaning and moaning, I crawl from my warm bed.
He clunks a pan of water on the stove,
adds a shake of salt, pours a stream of oatmeal.
I whine I'm not hungry.
He says he'll make a bit more anyway. . .just in case.

Postcards from the Old Man

I leisurely awaken in the bathtub,
Run more steaming heat in the suds to ease morning chills.
Pink and wrinkled, I crawl out, wipe down, robe up,
walk in shivers to the kitchen.
Clutching the milk, I pour white puddles
over the crusty glob of once-warm cereal,
sprinkle sugar and cinnamon on top.
After one sticky bite, I scrape it in the trash . . .

Dad comes in from outside, says it is "20 below ";
he's started both our cars to warm them up,
threw a shovel in the trunk for me. . .just in case. . .

He grabs his barn-shaped, black metal lunch box,
heads out to his foundry job
where after pouring hot molten lava,
he'll return home at exactly 5:30 . . .sooty black
to shovel steps and sidewalks,
laugh with the family over a game of 500.

Boon and Erickson bring me back to 1994
with another goofy sled dog joke.

I realize I never told Dad thanks
for starting my car on frigid winter mornings,
never sat down once to share a lonely bowl of cereal with him.
I press cruise up to 70 . . . just in case. . .

THE PARTING CHORUS

In front of Hotel Scott from left to right: Horace Webster, Mr. Robinson, Warner Smith, Curtis Shattuck, William Dixon, George Warner

"The Mississippi does not alter its
locality by cut-offs alone:
it is always changing its habitat bodily—
is always moving. . . "
-- Mark Twain, *Life on the Mississippi* --

Postcards from the Old Man

Clearwater is under a different watch now. Asa White, Alonzo Boyington, Simon Stevens, Thomas Porter, and many of the other early town founders would hardly recognize this little burg. Wannigans and trains no longer coast up and down the river's shores. The building still stands and is used as an apartment complex, but the town no longer has a school. Catholic parishioners, who had the second building since the town was incorporated, recently sold the church that was located on Spring Street and are planning to build a new one sometime in the future.

In addition, Main Street has seen some renovation in the last few years. Humble and picturesque, the United Methodist Church still stands, but the addition of a new fellowship hall added convenience and grace to the old structure. The Masonic Temple still glares at the rest of the town, but not so vacantly now because the Great River Educational Arts Theatre has brought some of this building back to life with its frequent children's plays. Phillips' Drug Store and Post Office, later becoming Kniss' Fairway Foods, no longer serves the community in food or pharmaceuticals, but the false-front and bay-like windows remain. The carpenter's restoration inside and a fresh coat of white paint outside bears promise that the soon-to-be apartment house will once again bring the building back to life.

Nowadays, all the action is on the hill. My mom's café, Dick's Lunch, has been replaced by a car wash and gas station. The main roads leading through Clearwater have changed, too. What once used to be the main route through town, Highway 152, has become Highway 75. A mini-mall houses a hardware, a grocery store, and a furniture store. A bank, a clinic, and a restaurant are nearby. And while the Burbank Stage Company doesn't get the credit for advancing the village's economy, the state of Minnesota does for constructing Interstate 94. Nelson Brothers' Truck Stop and Restaurant, a motel, gas station, and a king and queen of fast food, Burger King and Dairy Queen have awakened this sleepy village.

Mark Twain wrote in *Eruption* that "Distance lends enchantment to the view." Like all towns, large and small, Clearwater was made up

The Parting Chorus

of all types of memorable characters. The longer I am away, the more I want to forget about certain individuals who may have caused me problems. I choose to focus on the places I lived in and around Clearwater, the town's wonderfully historic buildings, and its memorable people who gave me story material.

This bend in the Old Man may be shallower than others, but it still anchors me. No matter how many times I meander away, when I become lonely, I hop on my raft and pilot my way back.

Postcards from the Old Man

A GENEALOGIST VISITS THE BELIEVERS FROM MASSACHUSETTES BAY COLONY

I thought I'd have a spiritual reunion here,
feel my DNA tug and pull me back
to the dust and ashes of my ancestors' lives.
Even Cape Ann's whales provide clues to where they've been:
flute prints, waves flattened to odd-shaped circles,
help watchers trace their paths.
But these mammals are alive; my Puritan kin lie scattered
in dark, elm-shrouded cemeteries in Williamstown, Lynn, Chelmsford
and other villages up and down this eastern seashore.

While living, the pious led lives of simplicity:
plowing, planting, cooking, weaving.
They sidestepped verdant forests where Old Scratch lived,
fearing he'd sweep them up in his tricks.
They knew his traps:
milking on Sunday, conjuring up spirits, reading unholy books.
A sneeze could prove demonic.
Their only compasses, a few Bibles and the "elect,"
steered most on course, save for the unfortunate few:
John Proctor, Giles Corey, Rebecca Nurse.

Like breakers upon rock, their tidal convictions washed and waned.
Some of my lucky relatives, heretics I suppose,
cast away on less turbulent tides to new havens—
Connecticut, Rhode Island, Vermont.
Eventually, their descendents traveled further inland
to landlocked farms in Iowa, Minnesota, Dakota.
These pilgrims sail closer to my genetic pool.

While vacationing in Massachusetts,
I wear the hat of a tourist,
wade in icy Oak Bluff Bay,
dig through wet sand for crystal-like quartz and pearly clam shells,
feel the salty dryness on my hands and feet the rest of the day.
But these trips do not provide a deep calling unto deep,
nor a murky illumination connecting me to these coastal harbors.
I've set my anchor in the Midwest—
no need for a lighthouse on my prairie.

www.ingramcontent.com/pod-product-compliance
Lightning Source LLC
Chambersburg PA
CBHW050822160426
43192CB00010B/1865